REAPPRAISING THE MUNICH PACT

REAPPRAISING THE MUNICH PACT
Continental Perspectives

Edited by Maya Latynski
With an introduction by John R. Lampe

The Woodrow Wilson Center Press
Washington, D.C.
The Johns Hopkins University Press
Baltimore and London

Editorial Offices
The Woodrow Wilson Center Press
370 L'Enfant Promenade, S.W.
Suite 704
Washington, D.C. 20024-2518 U.S.A.

Order from:
The Johns Hopkins University Press
701 West 40th Street
Suite 275
Baltimore, Maryland 21211-2190
Telephone 1-800-537-5487

Chapter 4 drawn from *The Soviet Union and Czechoslovakia, 1938–1948: The Foundations of Communist Rule and the Origins of the Cold War* by Michael Kraus. Forthcoming from Oxford University Press.

Printed in the United States of America
⊗ Printed on acid-free paper

9 8 7 6 5 4 3 2 1

Library of Congress Cataloging-in-Publication Data

Reappraising the Munich Pact : continental perspectives / edited by
  Maya Latynski ; with an introduction by John R. Lampe.
      p.   cm.
    Papers from a conference convened on October 27-28, 1988 in
  Washington, D.C. by the Woodrow Wilson International Center for
  Scholars.
    Includes bibliographical references and index.
    ISBN 0-943875-38-2 (cloth) : $17.50. — ISBN 0-943875-39-0 (paper)
  : $9.25
    1. Munich Four-Power Agreement (1938)—Congresses. 2. World War,
  1939-1945—Causes—Congresses. 3. World War, 1939-1945—Diplomatic
  history—Congresses. I. Latynski, Maya. II. Woodrow Wilson
  International Center for Scholars.
  D727.R43   1992
  940.53′112—dc20   91-45734
                                                              CIP

The Center is the "living memorial" of the United States of America to the
nation's twenty-eighth president, Woodrow Wilson. The U.S. Congress
established the Woodrow Wilson Center in 1968 as an international institute
for advanced study, "symbolizing and strengthening the fruitful relationship
between the world of learning and the world of public affairs." The Center
opened in 1970 under its own presidentially appointed board of directors.

In all its activities the Woodrow Wilson Center is a nonprofit, nonpartisan
organization, supported financially by annual appropriations from the U.S.
Congress, and by the contributions of foundations, corporations, and
individuals. Conclusions or opinions expressed in Center publications and
programs are those of the authors and speakers and do not necessarily reflect
the views of the Center staff, fellows, trustees, advisory groups, or any
individuals or organizations that provide financial support to the Center.

Woodrow Wilson International Center for Scholars
Smithsonian Institution Building
1000 Jefferson Drive, S.W.
Washington, D.C. 20560
(202) 357-2429

CONTENTS

ACKNOWLEDGMENTS

Support for this publication came from funds awarded to The Woodrow Wilson Center's East European Program by Congress under the terms of the Soviet and East European Research and Training Act of 1983. Funds for the conference came from congressional and Ford Foundation grants directly to the Center.

REAPPRAISING THE MUNICH PACT

INTRODUCTION

John R. Lampe

Few major events in modern European history have resisted reappraisal on their fiftieth anniversaries. In 1988, the infamous Munich Pact of 1938 was hardly an exception. The British and French agreement to German terms for annexing the Czech borderlands, without so much as consulting the government of Czechoslovakia, has for decades attracted more scholarly attention as a cause or starting point for World War II than any other diplomatic event of the 1930s.

Three September meetings between Hitler and British Prime Minister Neville Chamberlain culminated with the four-power agreement signed in Munich by Britain, France, Germany, and Italy on 30 September 1938. Its terms agreed to the German army's progressive occupation of five zones of the largely German Sudetenland of Czechoslovakia during the next ten days. Annexation to the Reich followed automatically. The government of Czechoslovakia was permitted to register its views only on the demarcation of the last zone. President Edvard Beneš and his associates had otherwise played no part in the pact that ceded to Hitler borderlands containing the Bohemian mountains and attendant Czech military fortifications.

The Nazi government joined in a guarantee that the new frontiers of Czechoslovakia would be respected. Hitler gave his public word on 26 September that this was "the last territorial demand I have to make in Europe." These assurances were honored for less than six months. On 15 March 1939, the German army crossed the recently truncated and much less defensible frontier in force, and Czechoslovakia ceased to exist as an independent state. British and French guarantees of Polish independence quickly followed but came too late and had too little credibility to mobilize enough opposition in or outside Germany to prevent the Nazi attack on Poland on 1 September 1939. Chamberlain found himself obliged to declare war less than one year after he had returned from Munich to tell a cheering airport crowd that the agreement he had signed with "Herr Hitler" promised "peace in our time"—surely the saddest and most ironic of all the fine phrases uttered by Western statesmen in the twentieth century.

Chamberlain had admittedly opened the way for the tragic appeasement at Munich in May 1938. He withheld assurances of support to the French government should it honor its obligation toward Czechoslovakia, when mobilization of Czechoslovak and German troops along their common border threatened a wider European war for the first time. Subsequent Czech concessions were offered with British encouragement to the Sudeten German party of Konrad Henlein during the summer of 1938, but they failed to move the führer. After all, he had told his top generals as early as 30 May that "it is my inalterable will to smash Czechoslovakia by military action in the near future."

A general European war did seem likely as autumn approached. Chamberlain flew twice to Germany to meet with Hitler. His missions to Berchtesgaden on 15 September and to Bad Godesberg on 22 September seemed to have failed. Then, Mussolini's proposal for a wider meeting in Munich coincided with British and French readiness to exclude any representatives of Czechoslovakia from such a conference. Hitler agreed and, as Gerhard Weinberg argues persuasively elsewhere in this volume, reluctantly accepted a peaceful solution to a problem that he had wanted to address by committing the German army to action.

Following the end of World War II, scholarly treatment of the Munich Pact began with traditional diplomatic history and moralistic criticism of French and, especially, British policy, which was personified by the naive or perfidious appeaser, Neville Chamberlain. More recent Western treatments have taken less traditional and less critical views. Instead, emphasis on the domestic play of British party politics as well as on the constraints of Britain's fragile economic recovery has provided some powerful, if not fully persuasive, evidence for how little British policy might have changed had not the "very one man," Neville Chamberlain, been prime minister. German scholars such as Bernd-Jürgen Wendt and Gustav Schmidt have joined British historians in exploring this structural approach.[1] This is, however, an approach that perpetuates the overemphasis on British behavior at Munich that evolved during the first two decades after World War II.

Throughout the 1960s, on one side of the Atlantic, the publication of the cabinet proceedings from the few years preceding the Munich Conference kept alive the Churchillian position of moral outrage initiated in 1948 by John Wheeler-Bennett.[2] On the other side of the Atlantic, American debates over postwar foreign policy frequently referred to and sometimes revolved around a Munich analogy to British behavior in the face of threatened aggression. U.S. administrations raised the analogy unsuccessfully with public opinion over Vietnam but successfully in the recent Gulf War. In scholarly discourse about the Munich Pact, even the full-scale reemergence of German scholarship has not broken the concentration on the British role. Witness the papers from a major conference of the 1980s, "The Fascist Challenge and the Policy of Appeasement," now published in the previously mentioned Mommsen volume. Despite its German editors, and authors from France, West Germany, the United States, and Great Britain, nearly two-thirds of its pages are at least partly devoted to British policy. Virtually none treats Czechoslovak or Polish policy. Fewer than one-third treat German, French, and Soviet policy.

The East and West European Program of The Woodrow Wilson International Center for Scholars, therefore, organized its conference on "The Munich Pact after Fifty Years: Reappraising Causes and Consequences" around the relatively neglected policies of these countries, before, during, and after the event. The conference, held in Washington, D.C., on 27–28 October 1988, provided a forum for presenting and discussing papers on German, French, and Soviet policy, respectively, by Gerhard Weinberg, William Rand Kenan, Jr., Professor of History, University of North Carolina, John Dreifort, Professor and Chair of the Department of History, Wichita State University, and Michael Kraus, Associate Professor of Political Science, Middlebury College. It also enabled an examination of the Munich Pact from Czechoslovak and Polish viewpoints. Joseph Zacek, Professor of History, State University of New York at Albany, traced the evolution of the pact's postwar historiography in Czechoslovakia. Anna Cienciala, Professor of History, University of Kansas, prepared a comparable piece on Poland to be included in this volume.

NOTES

1. Gustav Schmidt, "The Domestic Background to British Appeasement Policy," and Bernd-Jürgen Wendt, " 'Economic Appeasement'—A Crisis Strategy," in *The Fascist Challenge and the Policy of Appeasement,* Wolfgang J. Mommsen and Lothar Kettenacher, eds. (London, 1983), 101–24 and 157–73. Among British works see Maurice Cowling, *The Impact of Hitler, British Politics and British Policy, 1933–1940* (London, 1978); Paul Kennedy, "Appeasement and British Defense Policy in the Interwar Years," *British Journal of International Studies* 4 (1978):161–77; K. Middlemas, *Diplomacy of Illusion: The British Government and Germany, 1937–1939* (London, 1972); Alice Teichova, *An Economic Background to Munich: International Business and Czechoslovakia, 1918–1938* (London, 1974).
2. John W. Wheeler-Bennett, *Munich: Prologue to Tragedy* (New York: Macmillan, 1948); Jan Colvin, *The Chamberlain Cabinet: How the Meeting at 10 Downing Street 1937–1939 Led to the Second World War* (New York, 1971).

CHRONOLOGY OF THE MUNICH CRISIS

1933 Jan. 30 Hitler becomes chancellor of Germany.

1935 May 16 Czechoslovakia and Soviet Union sign a mutual assistance pact.

May 19 Pro-Nazi Sudeten Party makes electoral gains in Czechoslovakia.

Dec. 13 Beneš succeeds Masaryk as president of Czechoslovakia.

1936 Mar. 8 German troops reoccupy the demilitarized Rhineland in violation of the Treaty of Versailles.

1937 Oct. 17 Riots in Sudeten area of Czechoslovakia.

Nov. 5 Hitler informs his generals in Hossbach memorandum that Austria and Czechoslovakia will be annexed as the first stage in creating a *Lebensraum* for Germany.

Nov. 29 Sudeten Party secedes from Czech Parliament following a ban on its meetings.

1938 Mar. 13 Austria is declared part of Hitler's Third Reich.

Mar. 28 Hitler encourages German minority in Czechoslovakia to make demands that will break up the state.

Apr. 24 Germans in Sudetenland demand full autonomy.

Apr. 29 Britain reluctantly joins France in diplomatic effort on behalf of the Czechoslovak government.

May 9 Russia promises to assist Czechoslovakia in the event of a German attack, if Poland and Romania will permit the passage of Russian troops. Both, however, refuse.

May 18–21 German troop movements reported on Czech border; Czechoslovak government calls up reservists 20 May; partial mobilization 21 May.

May 22 Britain warns Germany of dangers of military action, but makes it clear to France that it is not in favor of military action itself.

Aug. 3 Walter Runciman visits Prague on mediation mission between Czechs and Sudeten Germans.

Aug. 11   Under British and French pressure, Czechoslovak Prime Minister Beneš opens negotiations with the Sudeten Germans.

Aug. 12   Germany begins to mobilize.

Sept. 4   Henlein, leader of the Sudeten Germans, rejects Beneš's offer of full autonomy and severs relations with the Czechoslovak government 7 Sept.

Sept. 7   France calls up reservists.

Sept. 11   Poland and Romania again refuse to allow the passage of Russian troops to assist Czechoslovakia.

Sept. 12   Hitler demands that Czechs accept German territorial claims.

Sept. 13   Unrest in Sudetenland quashed by Czech troops.

Sept. 15   Chamberlain visits Hitler at Berchtesgaden. Hitler states his determination to annex the Sudetenland on the principle of self-determination.

Sept. 18   Britain and France decide to persuade the Czechs to relinquish territory in areas where more than half of the population is German.

Sept. 20–21   Germany completes invasion plans. The Czech government initially rejects the Anglo–French proposals, but accepts them on 21 September.

Sept. 22   Chamberlain meets Hitler at Bad Godesberg. Hitler demands immediate occupation of the Sudetenland and announces 28 September for the invasion. The Czech cabinet resigns.

Sept. 23   Czechoslovakia mobilizes; Russia promises to support France in the event that it aides the Czechs.

Sept. 25   France and Britain threaten Hitler with force unless he negotiates.

Sept. 26   Partial mobilization of France.

Sept. 27   The Royal Navy is mobilized.

Sept. 28   Hitler delays invasion for twenty-four hours pending a four-power conference at Munich.

Sept. 29   At the Munich Conference, Chamberlain, Daladier, Hitler, and Mussolini agree to transfer the Sudetenland to Germany, while guaranteeing the remaining Czechoslovak frontiers.

Sept. 30   Hitler and Chamberlain sign the "peace in our time" communiqué.

Oct. 1   Czechs cede Teschen to Poland. Germany begins occupation of Sudetenland.

Oct. 5   Beneš resigns.

Oct. 6–8   Slovakia and Ruthenia are granted autonomy.

1939 Mar. 14   At Hitler's prompting, the Slovak leader Jozef Tiso proclaims a breakaway "Slovak Free State."

Mar. 15   German troops march into Prague and occupy Bohemia and Moravia.

Mar. 31   Britain and France promise aid to Poland in the event of a threat to Polish independence.

Aug. 25   Anglo–Polish mutual assistance pact signed in London. Hitler makes a "last offer" on Poland and postpones his attack until 1 Sept.

Sept. 1   German forces invade Poland and annex Danzig. Britain and France demand their withdrawal.

Sept. 3   Britain and France declare war on Germany.

Source: Chris Cook and John Stevenson, *The Longman Handbook of World History since 1914* (London: Longman's, 1991), 38–43.

1

Germany and Munich

Gerhard L. Weinberg

Looking back today on German policy toward Czechoslovakia in 1938, one can see some aspects of that policy more clearly than was possible in the past. This chapter initially summarizes what recent scholarly research reveals about certain critical questions regarding the background and nature of the Munich agreement. Then, it indicates which portions of the recently revealed information the German government did not know at the time. Finally, it describes the lessons that the German government, and especially Adolf Hitler himself, learned from what others then and since have considered a great German triumph, but which Hitler regretted at the time and eventually considered his greatest mistake.[1]

The German government from the beginning contemplated the destruction of Czechoslovakia. The more one learns about National Socialist foreign policy, the clearer this point becomes in retrospect. In an age that stressed the importance of self-determination, however, this insight was by no means as obvious as it is now. It should be noted, however, that on the higher levels of the German government, there was an extraordinary degree of consensus on the issue of making Czechoslovakia disappear from the map of Europe. Even those civilian and military officials who argued with Hitler about his plans at the famous Hossbach Conference of November 1937 and on subsequent occasions invariably concentrated on the risks, not the advisability, of such a policy. The enthusiasm for crushing Czechoslovakia never approached that for destroying Poland, but there are no indications of any fundamental opposition to it.

It is now quite clear that the national principle—that is, the belief that a self-defined national minority that lives in a state dominated by people of a different nationality should be entitled to specific protection of its special rights—was never a serious concern in German dealings with the Czechoslovak state. The Sudeten Germans were perceived from first to last as instrumentalities that might help Germany in destroying Czechoslovakia—never as a people in need of assistance. The noise made by German propaganda and diplomats about the Sudeten Germans was designed to weaken resolution in the West, separate Czechoslovakia from any outside support, harden resolve in Germany itself, and provide an excuse for military action at the appropriate moment. The agitation was directed toward the public, both foreign and domestic, and was designed to obscure, rather than emphasize, the real German interest. That interest was never the fate of the 3.5 million people of German background living within Czechoslovakia—except insofar as they might be used in the additional army divisions, which, it was confidently anticipated, could be recruited from among them for employment in Germany's expected great war against the Western powers.

The secret instruction given by Hitler on 28 March 1938 to Konrad Henlein, the leader of the Sudeten Germans, to make unreasonable demands of the Prague government that could not possibly be granted, has often been quoted as a clear sign that Hitler did not really want an agreement either between Germany and Czechoslovakia or between Czechoslovakia and its German-speaking citizens. What has too frequently been ignored are the simultaneous instructions given Henlein to use his contacts in England to influence its government not to intervene. This portion of the directives to Henlein from Berlin indicates that Hitler then already expected to wage war against Czechoslovakia, but hoped to isolate it from any wider conflict. This was precisely the opposite of German interest in having international pressure exerted on an independent Czechoslovak state in favor of its Sudeten German citizens.

Literature on Munich customarily cites the diary of Alfred Jodl, by that time already a central figure in the military planning of the Third Reich, as a key source for German policy in the spring and summer of 1938. It disregards the fact that the entries for April, May, and June on Hitler's plans are definitely not contemporaneous entries. They are, rather, a subsequent reconstruction and insertion, prepared by Jodl himself almost certainly after 24 July 1938, by which time a great many things had changed. For this reason, these reconstructed entries should not be quoted, although they often are by such historians as Donald C. Watt, as proof of what Hitler and his advisers thought on the dates to which they are attributed. Instead, these entries reflect Jodl's perception of events weeks, and even months, later, which is clearly an important distinction. Once this is recognized, a number of apparent discrepancies in the sources and their interpretation are quickly resolved.[2] One can now accept as correct accounts of Hitler's explaining in early April

1938 to the newly appointed German ambassador to Italy, Hans Georg von Mackensen, that the Czechoslovak issue would be settled in a few months; Hitler's instructions on military planning to General Wilhelm Keitel, the recently appointed head of the high command of the armed forces and Hitler's immediate military subordinate, on 21 April, which assume the complete and permanent military occupation of Czechoslovakia; and his deduction after his trip to Italy in early May that it would be safe to launch an attack on Czechoslovakia in 1938.

In his memoirs, German State Secretary Ernst von Weizsäcker carefully omitted passages, which may now be found in his published papers, concerning the timing of the decision to invade Czechoslovakia. His omissions were designed to maintain in postwar retrospect the misleading impression that the decision to go to war against Czechoslovakia was reached after, and as a result of, the May 1938 crisis, when actually it predated that event and thus cannot be attributed to it. This fantasy has had a very long life, indeed, but it remains a fantasy. Hitler returned from his visit to Italy on 10 May confident that Italy would provide the diplomatic support that was all he wanted then, because he was certain of Germany's military head start over all others and conscious of his mortality through the fear of cancer that had induced him to write his last will on 2 May.[3] Hitler emphatically rejected the contrary position of the chief of staff of the German army, General Ludwig Beck, whose warning against attacking Czechoslovakia that year was presented to Hitler by the new commander in chief of the German army on or about 12 May. Hitler's dismissal of Beck's objections accurately reflects his earlier idea that his first war—one against Czechoslovakia—should start in 1938. Those who continue to believe that Hitler's decision to attack Czechoslovakia was made after the May crisis must explain the reason that General Beck, who was probably well informed, drafted a detailed set of arguments against an attack two weeks earlier on 5 May 1938.[4]

The crisis of the weekend of 19–22 May provoked rumors of an imminent German invasion of Czechoslovakia, which precipitated a partial mobilization of reserves inside Czechoslovakia and warnings from London to Berlin of possible complications if Germany made the move. This can, therefore, now be considered to have played an entirely different role from that assigned to it by various past and present apologists for German policy as well as by those who believe in the driven, rather than the driving, Hitler. The German dictator had already decided to launch an invasion later that year, and, as we now know, he was arranging the details of that attack when the weekend crisis temporarily disturbed his planning. The technical implications were promptly considered by the German planners; although minor changes had to be made and incorporated into the appropriate military directives, the basic decision had been made already.

The greatest long-term significance of the May crisis was the way in which it may have misled the government of Czechoslovakia into believing that it could depend upon permanent support from England and France, not only in the event of a sudden and unprovoked German invasion but also in the face of apparently more limited German demands. Whatever the reason, Prague failed to seize the diplomatic initiative from a position of strength by offering concessions to the Sudeten Germans—concessions that would have exposed the negotiating strategy of the latter and, thereby, clarified the real as opposed to the pretended aims of Berlin's policies. Instead, Prague inadvertently played into German hands by leaving the initiative to Henlein and his masters in Berlin.

Today, it remains difficult to understand how so experienced a diplomat as Edvard Beneš, then president of Czechoslovakia but, in effect, still the author of its major foreign-policy decisions, could have allowed Prague to remain so passive. If the fundamental issues at stake were left to be defined by Germany through its propagandistic and diplomatic focus on the fate of the Sudeten Germans, how did he expect the public in England, France, Canada, Australia, South Africa, and New Zealand to grasp their true significance? This is not to shift the responsibility for the fatal choices made by Berlin to anyone else—least of all to Prague. But, if the Czechoslovak authorities seriously expected democratically governed societies to assist them in a war with Germany, it was supremely important to clarify the need to accept the enormous sacrifices of yet another great war to at least some of the peoples expected to make them.

It is now understood that the unofficial Anglo–German contacts in the summer of 1938 underscored the rigidity of Hitler's determination to fight a war. The visits to London of Albert Forster, the leader of the Nazis in the Free City of Danzig, and of Fritz Wiedemann, Hitler's military adjutant, left Hitler entirely unmoved; the warnings about German intentions conveyed to London and Paris by Hitler's German opponents confused instead of enlightened their audiences. The latter point was recently inadvertently made more obvious in Marion Thielenhaus's book. Although it is extremely sympathetic to both von Weizsäcker and others, this volume offers a description of how, in the summer of 1938, they ended up working at cross purposes with one another.[5]

The truly critical problem of the potential role of the German armed forces can now also be viewed more clearly. The German air force and navy presented no problems. Hermann Göring, commander in chief of the air force, pushed forward as rapidly as possible, conscious of the risks of a wider war that would make him hesitant in the autumn. Admiral Erich Raeder, commander in chief of the navy exiled to an insignificant post, was the only high-ranking naval officer who warned against the precipitation of war that year. The new commander in chief of the army, Walther von Brauchitsch, was in a very different position. On the one hand, as has already been mentioned, his chief of staff General Beck warned against war, and there were obvious signs of widespread concern among other high-ranking officers. Von Brauchitsch, however, had sold himself and the army to Hitler for subventions to enable him to move into a new marriage: He had promised to open the army to increased National Socialist influence, and, because he had neither moral courage nor standards, could always be relied upon to defer to Hitler's preferences. His disastrous role in German history has not received the attention it deserves; assuredly, his first major act was to rally many skeptics within the military hierarchy to Hitler's side in the summer of 1938.[6]

With von Brauchitsch on his side, Hitler could, or thought he could, disregard the skeptics within his own government. Because he was exceedingly sensitive to what he believed had been the poor public relations of the German government of 1914 in staging Germany's entrance into that war, he now planned to improve the situation by staging incidents inside Czechoslovakia to provide an excuse for invasion. At one time—under the obvious influence of the 1914 Sarajevo assassination—he had mentioned cheerfully arranging the murder of the German minister in Prague, as he had once toyed with the idea of having the German ambassador or military attaché in Vienna murdered to provide an excuse for the occupation of Austria. Instead, he turned the staging of incidents over to the German minority inside Czechoslovakia. Among prospective allies, Poland's parallel policy, the possibility of building closer relations with Japan, and Italy's presumed willingness to join Germany outweighed Hungary's hesitancy—hesitancy that the German government tried hard to overcome and never forgave.

As for the Soviet Union, Berlin perceived it to be minimally important and gave it little attention in its planning in 1938. Immersed in the great purges, which had begun to have a serious effect on the Soviet armed forces in 1937, the Soviet Union was busy decapitating its own military mechanism. While the German government knew better than anyone that the charges of collusion with Berlin being leveled against the Red Army by Stalin's secret police were false, it could only rejoice at the double benefit that would accrue. First, the Soviet Union would be incapable of any serious projection of military power beyond its borders; second, the charges were guaranteed to discourage any foreign power that might weigh allying itself with the Soviet Union against Germany with the prospect of working with Soviet officers who would be shot as German agents the following week. No wonder State Secretary von Weizsäcker could write: "As long as Stalin makes himself as useful as he is doing at present, we really need not have any special military worries about him."[7]

The British government had watched the developing crisis with great apprehension. The question of whether or not the issue most prominent in the public eye—the Sudeten German question—would be settled peacefully or lead to war presented a terrible dilemma. The government's military advisers told the cabinet to do whatever necessary to postpone, if not completely avoid, conflict. The Dominions of the United Kingdom were making it absolutely clear to London that they would not fight alongside Britain if the Sudeten German question led to war, and there is now evidence that the German government was at least generally aware of these reservations. As the realities of German goals finally began to emerge in early September, after Prague had finally produced some substantial concessions, and as Paris panicked at the firmer stand by London, Prime Minister Chamberlain decided on one last desperate step to preserve peace. He would fly to Germany to try to arrange something to avoid war.

Startled by Chamberlain's offer to come to Germany, Hitler immediately feared that the war he intended might somehow be averted. He realized that circumstances might compel him to settle for an arrangement that was propagandistically defensible but that would fail to shield from Western interference what he actually intended—the destruction of Czechoslovakia. He could not afford either the domestic or the international repercussions of refusing to see the British prime minister. How could a fervent believer in the legend that Germany had lost World War I because of the collapse of its home front expect that home front to hold firm in a new war if he had turned away a public offer to negotiate? And how could other countries be expected to leave Czechoslovakia to its fate after he rebuffed an attempt at a settlement?

Hitler was, therefore, compelled to agree to receive the British prime minister, but all the evidence we now have indicates that a military, not a diplomatic, resolution of the crisis remained his goal. In the interval between his two meetings with the British prime minister at Berchtesgaden and Bad Godesberg, Hitler took a series of steps designed to avert what he considered the "danger" of a peaceful settlement. Czechoslovakia agreed to cede the German-inhabited territories to Germany, to which Britain and France, as Chamberlain reported at the Godesberg meeting, consented. As long as this appeared to be the critical issue, London and Paris made it clear to Prague that if it came to war and the Western powers won, those areas would also not be returned to Czechoslovakia. This was the situation from which Hitler tried to find an exit into war by making new demands that would make an invasion of Czechoslovakia plausible. Initially, this approach appeared to succeed. Even if the Hungarians remained unwilling to move, the Poles seemed eager to act against Czechoslovakia for a piece of the booty, and Hitler's newly organized squad of Sudeten German hoodlums could arrange the incidents he thought necessary as a pretext for war. All appeared to be ready for war, when Hitler decided to retreat.

Not only were most of Hitler's military and diplomatic advisers doubtful about the wisdom of launching an attack at this time for fear of a wider war that they thought would develop after a German invasion of Czechoslovakia, but his close political associates Joseph Goebbels and Hermann Göring had also expressed reservations to him. Moreover, the German public appeared to be unprepared for the ordeal of what would probably be a general war, as Britain and France appeared increasingly certain to intervene rather than remain aloof. As was previously mentioned, the issue of a cohesive home front was important for a leader who devoutly believed that it had been the crumbling of that front, not defeat in war, that produced the German collapse of 1918. A critical turning point came when, at the last moment, Hitler's one prospective major ally, Mussolini, revealed his doubts. Italian forces in Spain were hostages to fortune in that civil war, he had no direct interest in the question at hand, and he was aware of Italian unpreparedness. Therefore, Mussolini suggested that the diplomatic triumph for Germany implicit in the cession of the German-inhabited border areas of Czechoslovakia to Germany—the cession already agreed on by both the Western powers and Czechoslovakia itself—would be better for Germany than the all-out war that now appeared imminent. As surprised by this latest turn in Italian policy as he had been by Chamberlain's original offer to fly to Germany, Hitler abandoned his plan for immediate war and grudgingly agreed to a settlement by conference at Munich. Trapped to some extent by his own strategy of pretending to be concerned about the fate of the Sudeten Germans, he would settle for what Germany had publicly demanded rather than for the immediate attainment by war of actual German political aims.

If this is the current view of Berlin's handling of the sequence of events leading up to Munich, there were some facts, either not known or not understood then, that can now be clarified. It is true that the Germans realized that France was still reeling from the enormous casualties of World War I and was preoccupied with the most extreme internal difficulties and was, therefore, reluctant to fight another war for almost any cause. Hitler also appeared to be more confident of French abstention than were most of his associates, but there is absolutely no evidence of any German knowledge that the French government had informed Prague officially in July 1938 that France would not fight over the Sudeten issue in any circumstances.[8] For once, the proverbial Parisian sieve did not leak. What we now know from published French diplomatic documents had been kept secret from Berlin as successfully as from London—to say nothing of most historians of the Munich crisis. One can still find accounts that accept the assertion that French reluctance to support Czechoslovakia was owing to the uncertainty of British assistance. It is now known that the French government deliberately hid behind London's alleged reluctance and became positively hysterical the moment it learned that the British government was actually prepared to go to war in the event that Germany invaded Czechoslovakia—that France could, therefore, no longer pretend to be holding back for fear of being let down by Britain.[9]

On the other hand, Hitler did not until the last moment, if then, recognize the probability that an attack on Czechoslovakia would actually initiate a general war. Neither he nor his new foreign minister, Joachim von Ribbentrop, understood a key implication of London's considering as a real issue what for them was purely a propaganda pretext— the fate of the Sudeten Germans. This implied, of course, that if the fate of the Sudeten Germans was to be decisively affected by their German cultural identity, as contrasted with their formal citizenship, then in London's eyes the Czechs and Slovaks ought to have their fate determined by the fact that they were not Germans. In other words, the converse of reluctance to fight on the issue of the Sudeten Germans— if that issue truly existed—was a willingness to fight over a German invasion of Czechoslovakia that was clearly designed to annex that country's non-German inhabitants to the Third Reich. This divergence of perspectives contributed to Hitler's last-minute reversal on 28 September 1938, when it became evident that an invasion launched after Czechoslovakia had already agreed to concede the border areas to Germany would precipitate a general war. In addition, it obscured the probable reaction to any breach of the Munich agreement.

The fundamental difference between the use of alleged nationality grievances as a pretext for expansionist ambitions, on the one hand, and the belief that negotiated concessions to make state and nationality lines coincide might promote the peace of all peoples of Europe, on the other, also continued after Munich, precluding a subsequent German–

British accommodation. After the Germans violated the Munich agreement in March 1939, the British would not negotiate with them until an independent Czechoslovakia was restored, and, after the German attack on Poland in 1939, they would not negotiate until both Czechoslovakia and Poland had regained their independence. Because the German government would entertain neither possibility, there could be no new Anglo–German agreement. If the nationality issue were serious, it had to apply to Czechs, Slovaks, or Poles as well as Germans, and if it were not, there could be no basis for negotiations. Nothing has come to light to suggest that anyone in Berlin grasped this point after Munich.

Upset as he was over having been cheated of war in 1938, Hitler, as we now know, drew four conclusions from this setback. First, he was more determined than ever that Czechoslovakia be deprived of its independence. Czechoslovakia would be punished rather than rewarded for having agreed to Germany's public demands, escaping only briefly the fate that Germany had decided for it. Second, although such an operation against a helpless Czechoslovakia would now not require a war at all, the doubts that had surfaced during the 1938 crisis among the German public about any war would have to be removed through a deliberate internal propaganda campaign designed to whip up stronger resolution for military action on the home front. Hitler promptly set about inaugurating such a campaign, interestingly enough, in the midst of the violent anti-Jewish pogrom all over Germany in November 1938. As he explained to an assemblage of German newspapermen, the propagandistic assertion that the new Germany wanted nothing but peace had been a great asset in dealing with foreign powers, but there was always the danger that such assertions might be believed at home as well. Third, Hitler determined that he would now secure his eastern flank by subordinating Hungary and Poland to Germany so that he could safely launch a campaign against Britain and France who, he insisted, had bluffed him out of war in 1938. Fourth, in the course of preparing for a future war, he would not allow himself to be trapped in negotiations again, which he believed had happened in 1938.

When Hitler's effort to secure his eastern front for an attack on the West foundered on Poland's unwillingness to subordinate itself to Germany, he accordingly conducted his diplomatic preparations for a preliminary war against Poland to avoid any possibility of another peaceful settlement. There would be no negotiations with Poland all summer of 1939 as there had been with Czechoslovakia in 1938; and, to prevent their resumption, in the critical final weeks of the crisis in 1939, the German ambassadors to London and Warsaw were recalled from their posts and forbidden to return. This time, instigating incidents that would provide the pretext for war was entrusted not to the German minority in Poland—the special organization of Sudeten German hoodlums had run out of steam in Czechoslovakia at the last moment—but instead to the newly formed Reich Security Main Office in Berlin under its leader Reinhard Heydrich. And just to make sure they had the desired effect, the incidents would be staged not in Poland, where there was always the possibility of mistakes or interruptions, but in Germany, where, it was confidently assumed, the SS officer in charge could operate unhindered.

As for Hitler's one great worry in 1939, that someone would try to arrange a compromise, he would go to great lengths to avoid it.[10] A notorious incident occurred at the end of August 1939, when the British ambassador to Germany, Sir Nevile Henderson, almost came to blows with von Ribbentrop over the latter's refusal to hand over a set of the German demands on Poland. This situation resulted from Hitler's prior orders to his foreign minister that in no circumstances was he to give these demands to the British. The demands were designed to rally the German home front for war and to present Poland in a bad light to the West. The one thing the German government definitely did not want was to risk having the demands accepted.

Never again would Hitler change his mind about attacking another country once he had formed and expressed a decision to do so.[11] The way in which he projected his own weakness onto others—claiming after Munich that his advisers were weaklings for issuing their warnings, when he himself had held back rather than test the accuracy of their prediction that an attack would lead to a general war, which Germany was likely to lose—may help to explain why none of his subsequent decisions to initiate hostilities against another country was reversed. Circumstances might require postponements, but he was careful not to repeat what he considered a terrible mistake.

There is another point that, though small, is worth mentioning. In 1939 Hitler was so eager to go ahead that, at the end, when he found that he did not need all the time he had allowed for his last-minute effort to separate Poland from Britain and France, he went to war one day earlier than he had originally believed necessary. Better to begin a war a day early than risk another twenty-four hours of peace during which others might contrive to deprive Germany of the conflict he so ardently desired. In the north, the west, the southeast, the east, and against the United States across the Atlantic, once Hitler had decided on it, every extension of the war was implemented.

Germany accordingly drew one country after another into the war, but the hostilities followed a course unanticipated by Hitler. Looking back over the war's disastrous development from the ruins of Berlin in February 1945, he tried to discern what had gone wrong, how and where Germany's spectacular ascent to world domination had derailed. Munich was the explanation: "I ought to have seized the initiative in 1938," he asserted on 14 February 1945.[12] "We ought to have gone to war in 1938," he repeated a week later.[13] "September 1938 would have been the most favorable date. . . . We ought then and there to have settled our disputes by force of arms." It was all the fault of that "arch capitalist-bourgeois Chamberlain with his deceptive umbrella in his hand."

Whether or not Hitler's retrospective analysis is correct, it is essential for an understanding of German policy from October 1938 until the end of World War II to know that he quite consistently held such a view. Hitler drew his conclusions from these alleged "lessons of Munich," and, if they differ from those drawn by others, they are no less important. On the contrary, they must be assimilated into our examination of subsequent developments, if we are to understand these events and the impact of Munich upon them.

In his speech of 26 September 1938, Hitler had proclaimed to the world: "Wir wollen gar keine Tschechen" (We don't want any Czechs at all).[14] As we now know, by that he meant not what most listeners assumed—namely, that he wanted only the portion of Czechoslovakia inhabited by Germans—but, rather, that he expected to seize all of Bohemia and expel its Czech population. As we now also know, the hope of the Sudeten Germans expressed in their slogan, "Heim ins Reich" (Home to Germany), would be fulfilled after World War II in a manner few could have anticipated—by their expulsion from Czechoslovakia. As one looks back on the disasters that those years brought upon both the peoples of Czechoslovakia and the Germans, it should become increasingly clear that nations that have difficulties living side by side would be well advised to beware of the existence of much greater tragedies than having unpleasant neighbors. When the attempt to shift boundaries to match populations does not lead to a generally acceptable solution, there is always the terrible alternative of moving the populations to fit the boundaries. The Germans had brought this second procedure to Europe in a terrifying manner during World War II; at the end of it, it would be applied to the Germans themselves on a scale that dwarfs all prior population movements of which we are aware. Perhaps here, too, is a "lesson" of Munich worth pondering.

NOTES

1. Gerhard L. Weinberg, *The Foreign Policy of Hitler's Germany: Starting World War II, 1937–1939* (Chicago, 1980), 461–62.
2. Ibid., 337, n. 87; and 370, n. 219.

3. Gerhard L. Weinberg, ed., "Hitler's Private Testament of May 2, 1938," *Journal of Modern History* 27, no. 4 (December 1955): 415–19.

4. I have gone into quite a bit of detail here because the sequence of events in May 1938 has been seriously confused in many accounts that overlook the extent to which an accurate chronology is essential for the correct understanding of developments.

5. Marion Thielenhaus, *Zwischen Anpassung und Widerstand: Deutsche Diplomaten 1938– 1941* (Between conformity and resistance: German diplomats 1938–1941) (Paderborn, 1984).

6. It is not yet clear whether this action of Hitler's and the effect on von Brauchitsch is related to the subsequent extensive program of secret gifts and subventions to German generals and admirals in World War II.

7. See the reference in Weinberg, *Foreign Policy 1937–1939*, 190.

8. The relevant French documents are cited in ibid., 398.

9. Ibid., 423 and 428.

10. On this comment, see Winfried Baumgart, "Zur Ansprache Hitlers vor den Führern der Wehrmacht am 22. August 1939" (About Hitler's address to the leaders of the Wehrmacht on 22 August 1939), *Vierteljahrshefte für Zeitgeschichte* 16, no. 2 (August 1968): 120–40; 19, no. 3 (July 1971): 294–304.

11. It might be argued that the German idea to invade Switzerland in the summer of 1940 constitutes the one exception to this rule, but the available evidence on the plans for operation "Christmas Tree" (Tannenbaum) does not include any indication of an actual decision by Hitler to proceed with the attack. No precise date was ever set, and, hence, no formal postponement took place, either.

12. Hugh R. Trevor-Roper, ed., *The Testament of Adolf Hitler: The Hitler-Bormann Documents February-April 1945* (London: Cassell, 1961), 58. It should be noted that some questions have been raised, but not resolved, about the authenticity of these documents, especially by Professor Werner Jochmann of Hamburg. The comments they include on the Munich crisis are consistent with other known utterances of Hitler's, but a caveat is in order.

13. Ibid., 84.

14. Max Domarus, ed., *Hitler: Reden und Proklamationen 1928–1945* (Speeches and proclamations) (Neustadt a.d. Aisch: Verlagsdruckerei Schmidt, 1962), 732.

2

The French Role in the Least Unpleasant Solution

John E. Dreifort

On "Black Wednesday," 28 September 1938, Parisian concierges were calmly distributing sand to be used to fight fires started by the anticipated dropping of German incendiary bombs, and the streets were choked with traffic as thousands of Parisians desperately sought to evacuate the city. In England, with Neville Chamberlain's moving but melancholy broadcast of the night before ringing in their ears, Londoners continued to dig slit trenches in Hyde Park, and Chamberlain had begun to address the members of Parliament on the seriousness of the international situation. War, it seemed, was only two hours away.

Suddenly, a message was passed to the prime minister indicating Hitler's agreement to participate in a four-power conference to be held at Munich on the following day. As the dramatic news of the impending conference was broadcast, the pulse of Europe slowed noticeably, and confidence returned that war could be averted. Shortly thereafter, in the deep recesses of the British Foreign Office, Sir Philip Nichols, counselor in the central division, typed a note to his superior in which he suggested that should the Munich Conference produce recriminations between France and Britain: "We certainly here in the Foreign Office have sufficient evidence to make the position of certain members of the French government extremely unpleasant!" He went on to warn that the "washing of dirty Anglo–French linen" in public would, of course, be quite damaging to both countries, and asked whether some sort of agreement could be reached by the two powers "to let bygones be bygones so far as this kind of evidence is concerned."[1] Just what "evidence" he referred to is difficult, if not impossible, to know—indeed, it is not the objective of this chapter to ferret it out. What is important, however, is the fact that this statement touches on the crux of one of the fundamental questions surrounding the events leading to the Munich Conference and the subsequent betrayal of Czechoslovakia—what, in fact, was the nature of the Franco–British relationship during the period leading up to the conference, and how did it influence the path pursued and the decisions taken?

As French historian Henri Dutailly reiterated in one of the most recent studies of the interwar period, "there existed two established facts accepted by the great majority of political and military decision-makers: France could not survive another war of attrition ground out on her own soil"; and, "she did not possess on her own the financial, economic and demographic means to confront Germany."[2] Yet, the French security system erected with so much hope in the 1920s to offset this situation had begun to deteriorate, piece by piece, precisely when its need had become most obvious. Indeed, a major factor in the thinking of French policy makers during the September crisis that made Britain doubly important was their perception that there existed no viable alternative allies.

French leaders have been frequently criticized for failing to explore more seriously Soviet intentions and capabilities during the crisis. In fact, most prominent figures in the French government believed that Stalin hoped to take advantage of a Franco–German war—perhaps even provoke one—to promote an ideological revolution in Europe. Moscow's later professions aside, its intentions appeared dubious at best. More important in the immediate sense is that no military accord had been negotiated with the Soviets to give force to the Franco–Soviet Pact signed in 1935. French military analysts recognized the value of the vast Soviet manpower reserves and the large Soviet air force. The effect of Stalin's purges of the Soviet high command and pessimistic evaluations of Soviet equipment, however, more than offset any advantages that the Soviets might bring to a war over Czechoslovakia. Even geography mitigated against such an offensive action. The Soviets had no common frontier with either Germany or Czechoslovakia, and it was doubtful that Poland and Romania would permit Soviet ground forces to transit their territory to aid the Czechs. Without such forces being brought to bear, the Soviets could play only a secondary role in a conflict over Czechoslovakia. In any case, it was immaterial whether or not the Soviets could lend significant aid. The French believed that Moscow had no intention of involving itself and would use every available pretext for standing aside.[3]

Among the other potential sources of support, the prospects looked equally bleak to policy makers in Paris. If anything, Poland appeared more likely to line up against Czechoslovakia to seize the Teschen district if the opportunity arose. Italy had slipped from the category of ally to that of enemy. In fact, should war break out, the French high command had developed a plan to launch an attack against Libya under the assumption that Italy would automatically side with Germany. Deep-seated American isolationism prevented President Roosevelt from doing anything more than speaking out against the horrors of war, appealing for a negotiated settlement of the crisis, but announcing that "the United States has no political involvements in Europe." In response to rumors that the United States would enter a coalition to restrain Germany, Roosevelt publicly declared that they were "a hundred per cent wrong."[4]

In light of France's increasing diplomatic isolation, therefore, Britain became of paramount importance in French diplomatic and strategic thinking during the Czechoslovak crisis of September 1938. Because of new sources that have become available during the past decade, including the long-awaited volumes of the *Documents diplomatiques français, 1932–1939*, it is now possible, at last, to attempt a final analysis and assessment of the French role and the Franco–British relationship during the Munich crisis.[5]

The background to the fateful September crisis has been well treated elsewhere, and most students of the period are familiar with the sequence of events that led up to Munich.[6] Suffice it to say that the Czechoslovak problem, which had been brewing ever since the Austrian Anschluss of March 1938, exploded into a full-fledged crisis in September. The situation had become so grave that war seemed inevitable. Even President Edvard Beneš's dramatic agreement in early September to grant the initial Sudeten demands had led only to further demands and outright violence. Events now began to approach the inexorable climax. On 15 September, Chamberlain seized the initiative with a bold stroke that he had been considering for some time by flying to Berchtesgaden to negotiate with Hitler face to face.[7] Their meeting made it quite clear that the most important issue was whether Czechoslovakia would continue to exist in its entirety or as a truncated shadow of a state that would be subjected to the every whim of Nazi Germany. Central to this issue was the position of Czechoslovakia's most important ally—France.

France had a long-standing commitment to Czechoslovakia. The two states were bound by a treaty of alliance, supplemented by a corollary to the Locarno Pact of 1925, which provided for mutual assistance in the event of an unprovoked attack. Czechoslovakia actually had become the "eastern bastion" of France's security system. Although France's relationship with other members of the Little Entente had fluctuated considerably in the aftermath of the reoccupation of the Rhineland, Czechoslovakia and France had maintained their close ties.[8] But, with the advent of the Daladier government in April 1938, the French position became increasingly ambiguous. Daladier frequently repeated that France was determined to prevent the dismemberment of Czechoslovakia. At a meeting with Chamberlain in London on 28 April, Daladier had declared to the British that it was "a question of will." If concessions obtained from Prague failed to have the desired effect, France and Britain "must not allow the destruction of Czechoslovakia." France considered its alliance with Czechoslovakia of "vital importance," and was determined to "execute its obligations" toward that nation.[9] As late as 12 July, Daladier underscored his belief that France's engagements to Czechoslovakia were "sacred and immutable."[10]

Various statements and activities of Foreign Minister Georges Bonnet, however, created a lingering doubt in the minds of many about how far France would be willing to go to protect its eastern ally. At the time of the May 1938 crisis, Bonnet had suggested that, should Czechoslovakia become unreasonable, France might consider itself released from its obligations.[11] The clearest statement of Bonnet's attitude had come on 20 July, when he warned the Czech minister in Paris, Stefan Osuský, that "Czechoslovakia *must be well convinced that France, like England, will not go to war*" over the Sudeten affair (Bonnet's italics). Some analysts have interpreted this to be the official French position—one that the government did not alter throughout the crisis. The evidence does not support their case, however. Premier Daladier's notations on the document reveal a fundamental disagreement with Bonnet at this time, which implies that the foreign minister's views did not represent those of the cabinet or government. Significantly, however, although Daladier disagreed with the substance of the statement, there is no evidence that he sought to limit its impact by issuing a retraction.[12] Clearly, in any case, those with responsibility for formulation of French policy entered the September crisis with divided counsel concerning France's obligations to Czechoslovakia.

Britain itself had no obligations toward Czechoslovakia except within the framework of the moribund League of Nations, and Chamberlain had scrupulously avoided committing Britain to act on behalf of that "faraway country." Britain, however, had a commitment to help maintain the security of France as part of the Locarno Agreement, and, in the aftermath of the Rhineland crisis, it had reaffirmed its guarantee of assistance in the event of unprovoked aggression against it by Germany.[13] The very question of what constituted unprovoked aggression was a ticklish one, but, try as they might, the French did not obtain a satisfactory clarification of the British position. The best they could get from London was Chamberlain's abstruse statement (and one to which the British repeatedly returned) of 24 March: "If war broke out . . . it would be quite impossible to say where it would end and what Governments would be involved."[14]

During the summer of 1938, despite concerns being expressed by French representatives in Berlin and Prague, the Daladier government's position had remained determinedly passive—waiting, in the words of Emile Charvériat, deputy director for political affairs at the foreign ministry, "for the results of the Runciman mission."[15] Therefore, as the war clouds began to loom in September, the precise nature and spirit of Franco–British–Czech commitments remained quite obscure. On 8 September, Sir Eric Phipps, the British ambassador in Paris, reported that Daladier had declared that "France will march to a man" should Germany cross the Czech frontier.[16] Yet, a few days later, Phipps reported that Daladier was showing signs of weakening and seeking to avoid facing up to France's obligations.[17] For his part, Lord Halifax, the British foreign secretary, muddied the waters still further. On 10 September, Bonnet had asked Phipps, not as an ambassador but as a friend, what Britain's response would be to a question from France in the event of a German attack on Czechoslovakia: "We are going to march, will you march with us?" Halifax, in a masterly piece of diplomatic obfuscation, replied: "While His Majesty's Government would never allow the security of France to be threatened, they are unable to make precise statements of the character of their future action . . . in circumstances that they cannot foresee."[18] It was potentially a devastatingly obscure statement, but, as Phipps noted, Bonnet seemed pleased with its essentially negative nature.[19] In any event, as they entered the final hectic two weeks of the crisis, the fundamental questions of how far France would support Czechoslovakia and how Britain would interpret its commitment to France remained unresolved and became the focal point of French decision making during the remainder of the crisis.

In the aftermath of Hitler's harangue at Nuremberg on 12 September, which precipitated a serious outbreak of violence in the Sudetenland, Daladier's government could no longer allow matters to slide. Yet, at a cabinet meeting on 14 September, a serious split in the government became apparent. Daladier favored a strong course, leading, perhaps, to partial mobilization. He was opposed, however, by Bonnet and several others in the cabinet, who insisted that failure to prepare French public opinion for war and the weakness of the air force made such a course impossible.[20] Nevertheless, Daladier took the initiative on the afternoon of the thirteenth to propose to Britain the convocation of a three-power conference of France, Britain, and Germany "to safeguard all possibilities of an amicable settlement." He warned that events in Czechoslovakia might quickly pass them by, leaving France to confront its obligations: "It is important to make all efforts to stop this dangerous evolution."[21] On the same day, however, Bonnet visited the British ambassador, Sir Eric Phipps, "with emotion" telling him "that at no price should we allow ourselves to be involved in war without having weighed all the consequences and having measured in particular the state of our military forces."[22] This performance hardly presented the British with a united front, which Chamberlain quickly detected. Much to Daladier's dismay, the British response brushed aside his call for a three-power conference. Instead, on 14 September at 3:20 A.M., Phipps telephoned Daladier to tell him that Chamberlain was "studying . . . another possibility of direct action in Berlin."[23] Late that evening, Phipps informed Daladier that Chamberlain's meeting with Hitler at Berchtesgaden had been arranged for the following day. Clearly, Chamberlain had displayed precious little concern for French sensitivities as he developed his plan to visit Hitler. Just as clearly, too, Daladier was miffed. Phipps reported: "Daladier did not look very pleased after I had delivered my message." The French premier wished Chamberlain well but pointedly reminded Phipps that he had earlier proposed a conversation "à trois."[24] Bonnet, however, hailed the meeting, praising Chamberlain's "exceptional initiative" in engaging his "moral authority and public responsibility in the service of peace." The foreign minister took the opportunity to stress Franco–British solidarity, which "remains necessary more than ever."[25]

For the next three days, the French could do little but await the results of the Hitler–Chamberlain talks. The Czechs, similarly in the dark and fearing the worst, could not have been encouraged by signs coming from Paris. On 16 September, Bonnet told Osuský that French public opinion was "profoundly pacifist" and that it desired a peaceful resolution to the crisis. Moreover, he warned the Czech minister, "there was no question of France marching in this if she did not have a complete agreement on all points with Great Britain." In a harbinger of things to come, Bonnet made a "suggestion" that the Czechs consider ceding to Germany those areas that were entirely Sudeten in return for a great-power guarantee for the frontiers of the new Czech state. Leaving no doubt as to the nature of this "suggestion," Bonnet "earnestly requested . . . [Beneš] not to continue in the illusions in which he had lived for so many months."[26] On the following day, the embattled Beneš submitted a proposal to Paris that would cede three areas containing 800,000–900,000 Germans, while leaving key fortifications and more than a million Germans in Czech lands.[27]

Upon hearing Hitler's demands at Berchtesgaden, Chamberlain had stalled by indicating that he could not give a categorical reply until he had consulted with both his government and his French ally. After

Chamberlain returned to London, however, it was decided at a meeting of his "inner group" of advisers[28] not to send France any news of the Berchtesgaden discussions, "as the only result would be that the gist . . . would immediately become known all over the world."[29] At a meeting of the full cabinet on the following day, Halifax disclosed that the French government had been told only that "the Prime Minister had found the situation critical" and that Hitler had pressed for acceptance of self-determination.[30] Meanwhile, however, a dispatch had been received from Phipps indicating that the French were "much disturbed" by not being informed about the results of the Berchtesgaden meeting. Phipps had asked that Daladier and Bonnet be invited to London to receive this information.[31] In a supreme bit of irony that cut right to the core of the question of obligations and responsibility, Halifax warned the cabinet that "there was great danger that the responsibility . . . might be placed on our shoulders, although it was the French and not we ourselves who had treaty obligations with the Czechoslovak Government."[32] After seizing the initiative and undertaking direct negotiations with Hitler, without bothering to consult with the French beforehand, the question of ultimate responsibility for the betrayal of Czechoslovakia had finally hit home, and Halifax now sought a means to shift the blame from Britain's shoulders. Chamberlain thought that "if the French asked us our opinion, we should reply that it was France which was primarily involved, but that we thought they would take a wise course if they said that they would not fight to prevent the self-determination of the Sudeten Germans." It was finally agreed that the French would be invited to London for a meeting the next day, although Halifax cautioned his colleagues that "we should avoid allowing the French to say that they came to London and found that we had decided to give the show away."[33] In any event, the visit would be useful for drawing out the French position.

On the morning of 18 September, Daladier, Bonnet, and their "circus," as Sir Alexander Cadogan of the Foreign Office described their entourage,[34] flew to London and began a marathon session with the British ministers.[35] After hearing Chamberlain's description of his conversations with Hitler, Daladier, undoubtedly miffed at the belated invitation, speaking "with a voice trembling with carefully modulated emotion," explained France's position, firmly stressing its obligations and honor.[36] "The obligations contracted by France are clear and inevitable," he said. Moreover, despite suggestions that had appeared in some French newspapers, no Frenchman would "commit such a crime" of deserting an ally. Nevertheless, Daladier admitted that the French delegations had come to London to seek a peaceful solution to the crisis confronting Europe. As Chamberlain later related to the cabinet, Daladier then stated:

> They were anxious to hear the views of the British Government, who had by now had some days to deliberate over their position. To this, the Prime Minister had replied that, since the French were bound by treaty obligations and we were not, he thought that it was for the French to express their views first. The French representatives in turn had found some means of passing the ball back into our court, and so matters had continued during the whole morning.

This bit of buck passing merely reflected the woeful attempt by both sides to avoid committing themselves to or having to assume responsibility for the decisions that would follow. Cleverly, each side tried to draw out the other's position without revealing its own. Finally, the British, as Cadogan put it, were able to bring Daladier "back to earth," and the French premier defined the problem as one of preserving peace while retaining as much of Czech independence as possible.[37] During lunch, the tensions began to ease, and the afternoon discussions became more productive. Daladier opposed the principle of self-determination—it would raise the question of other minorities—but was willing to consider some form of outright transfer of territory. He was reluctant, however, to urge this upon the Czechs unless a revamped system of guarantees also could be extended to them. After all, Daladier warned, "Hitler's real aim was the domination of Central and South-Eastern Europe, and that, for this purpose, he was anxious to secure the total dismemberment of Czechoslovakia." Therefore, Daladier asked Britain to give a fresh guarantee to the remainder of Czechoslovakia. Leslie Hore-Belisha, British secretary of state for war, believed that at this time Daladier had Chamberlain "up against it."[38] But Chamberlain did not allow the French an easy victory, arguing that such a guarantee "involved a very serious additional liability" for Britain. He also indicated the impossibility of Britain's effectively fulfilling such a guarantee if Czechoslovakia were actually invaded. But the French persisted and pressed for a definite commitment. After Chamberlain called for a brief adjournment to consult with his advisers, the British finally agreed to a general guarantee, conditional upon Czechoslovakia's acceptance of an Anglo–French plan of transfer of territory as well as a neutral stance in matters of foreign affairs. Chamberlain then put the hard question to Daladier: What would happen if Beneš refused to go along with the joint Anglo–French proposal? After waffling a bit, Daladier indicated that he did not think such a reply would be possible. "The strongest pressure would have to be brought to bear on Dr. Beneš to see that the Czechoslovak Government accepted the solution proposed by the French and British Governments."

Although it has been argued that Daladier won an important concession from Chamberlain, it is clear that the Englishman was the victor in this particular battle. Sir John Simon, perhaps Chamberlain's most avid supporter in the cabinet, told his colleagues: "The French Ministers on arrival had been somewhat woebegone, but they had gone away with heart and courage restored to them by the Prime Minister."[39] In fact, however, the record shows that Daladier had come in like a lion and had gone out like a lamb. Although he had finally secured a British continental commitment and avoided the use of a plebiscite to delimit areas to be surrendered to Germany, he had made major concessions to Chamberlain. Indeed, some details of the Franco–British guarantee still had to be worked out; yet, Daladier, after a rather testy start, had swung around to adopt Chamberlain's view about the need for Czechoslovak concessions. Moreover, the crucial question of how Britain interpreted its commitment to France had gone unresolved—indeed, it had gone almost unmentioned. Finally, Daladier had agreed to continue to allow Chamberlain to carry the ball in negotiations with Hitler. As the French historian René Girault has argued, after 18 September, by leaving its Czechoslovak ally in the hands of British arbitration, "the French decision-makers opened the path which, in a few days, would lead them to Munich."[40] Nevertheless, and even better from the British point of view, as Samuel Hoare, another of Chamberlain's closest confidants, put it, "The decisions taken were joint decisions for which we could not be saddled with the major share of responsibility."[41]

Upon their return to Paris, the Frenchmen faced the task of selling the Anglo–French plan to the cabinet. There had been no discussion of this matter by the full council of ministers prior to the meeting in London—perhaps for fear that divisions already apparent would develop into a full-blown ministerial crisis precisely as had happened during the Anschluss five months earlier. Such a crisis could leave France without a government at a critical moment. Nevertheless, despite predictable opposition from Paul Reynaud, Georges Mandel, and a few others, the council of ministers fell in line behind Daladier and approved the plan, while delaying any discussion of what to do should Czechoslovakia reject the plan.[42]

It fell to Bonnet to break the news to the unfortunate Osuský. He did so in no uncertain terms. He outlined for the Czech minister the essence of the Anglo–French discussions in London and presented the details of the plan developed at the meeting. An emotional Osuský was told that the Anglo–French plan represented the "least unpleasant solution" available at the moment. To add emphasis to his statement, Bonnet reminded the Czech of his earlier statements of June and July. Now, in a blatant half-truth, he warned Osuský that the British "have in effect informed us that if Prague refused, it could only disassociate itself from the dispute." France would then be forced to "appraise *closely* the situation." It was certain that in these conditions, "the assistance that France could lend to Czechoslovakia could have no effectiveness if it were not completed by English solidarity."[43] The British connection obviously remained paramount, and Prague would not be permitted to upset their relationship by belligerently dragging France into a war on behalf of 3,500,000 Sudeten Germans. Bonnet's attitude had not changed since July, but Daladier's position in all of this still remained uncertain.

A week later, after pressuring Beneš into capitulating only to find out at Godesberg that Hitler had raised the price of surrender, the French and British again found themselves conferring in London. They were now confronted with a demand for the occupation of the Sudetenland by 1 October. It was a decisive moment for France and Britain.

This time, Chamberlain did not delay in inviting the French ministers.[44] Now, however, Daladier made the British wait, while he consulted with his council of ministers in the morning before leaving for London. Only the scantiest record exists of the meeting, but, despite subsequent claims by Daladier and Bonnet that the group unanimously rejected the German demands, it is clear from other participants that serious divisions existed. The most likely scenario appears to have been that Reynaud, Mandel, and a few others advocated a strong stance. Indeed, Reynaud apparently declared that "the Godesberg terms are the end of Czechoslovakia." These "resisters" were undoubtedly opposed by Bonnet, Camille Chautemps, Guy La Chambre, and others. Daladier was probably somewhere in the middle. Adhering to the pattern followed after the London conference a week earlier, the declaration of unanimity was simply for public consumption or, in this case, perhaps to strengthen Daladier's hand in London.[45]

Meanwhile, Chamberlain busied himself with plans for maintaining Britain's vague position vis-à-vis France during the forthcoming talks. He proposed to the cabinet that they remind the French that "we should not say that if [Hitler's] proposals were rejected, we undertook to declare war on Germany. Equally, we should not say that if the proposals were rejected we should in no circumstances declare war on Germany." After all, the responsibility for acceptance or rejection of the German proposals lay with Czechoslovakia and, indirectly, France. Britain, Chamberlain maintained, was "merely acting as an intermediary."[46] Once again, it would first be necessary to extract a commitment from the French.

Yet, when the meeting finally began at nine o'clock on Sunday evening, 25 September, less than thirty-six hours after Chamberlain's return from Godesberg, the prime minister's carefully delineated plans were thwarted. In a meeting that Lord Strang described as "among the most painful which it has been my misfortune to attend,"[47] Daladier again opened on the offensive: "In the view of the French government, it was no longer a question of reaching a fair arrangement. Hitler's object was to destroy Czechoslovakia and to dominate Europe." Chamberlain jumped at the opening. What would France do if Hitler refused to compromise? Daladier replied: "In that case each of us will have to do our duty." And how would France presume to do that—by an invasion of Germany? Daladier, on less firm ground when it came to the military realities, had heard enough and retorted: "I would consider it ridiculous to mobilize the French land forces only to leave them . . . doing nothing in their fortifications. It would be equally ridiculous to do nothing in the air." Daladier tried to defuse concerns about overwhelming German air superiority by pointing out that, although General Franco had enjoyed total control of the air during the Spanish Civil War, it had not won the war for him. The French premier also noted that Hitler's Siegfried Line was "a lot less solid than he pretends."[48] Finally, Daladier reversed the tables and put the hard questions to Chamberlain. Did Britain accept Hitler's plan? Would they press it on the Czechs? Did they think France should take no action? And so it went.[49] As one scholar has described it, "They wrangled, like men fighting in a dark alley, searching for each other's weakness."[50]

At the same time, of course, they cleverly refrained from revealing too much about their own plans. At one point, however, the ambivalence of Daladier revealed itself. He suggested that since Hitler had objected to delays caused by the use of international commissions to delimit the boundaries of territories to be ceded, "Why not design a commission in three days, which would be able to finish its task in ten days, and, without waiting, authorize the immediate occupation by German troops of those districts where the Germanic majority is particularly important?" Hoare eagerly seized the proposal, which to him contained the seeds of a compromise that would permit France and Britain to retain some of the initiative, while allowing Hitler the rapid transfer of territories that he wanted. Chamberlain rebuffed the proposal. The prime minister reiterated that in light of his "experience" in recent conversations with Hitler, the latter wanted an immediate settlement. If there had been any possibility that such a plan would be acceptable, did not the French think that he would have pursued it? In fact, of course, four days later at Munich, the participants agreed to a plan that essentially adhered to Daladier's proposal rejected by Chamberlain on the twenty-fifth. The grueling session adjourned at midnight after having agreed that General Maurice Gamelin, general chief of staff, would attend the next day.[51]

On the following day, Daladier and Chamberlain conferred alone before Gamelin was called in to present an analysis of the military situation. Daladier's strong stand the night before, along with increasing rumblings of discontent in the British cabinet, apparently had led to a change of heart for Chamberlain.[52] The prime minister told Daladier about a message that he was sending to Hitler through Sir Horace Wilson, his closest adviser, which included a final plea to Hitler to negotiate a solution to the crisis. If Hitler replied unfavorably, then Wilson was to tell him, "The French government have informed us that, if the Czechs reject the Memorandum and Germany attacks Czechoslovakia, they will fulfill their obligations to Czechoslovakia. Should the forces of France in consequence become engaged in active hostilities against Germany, we shall feel obligated to support them."[53] Here, finally, was the firm statement of support that France had for so long tried to extract. If Chamberlain had anticipated a great outburst from Daladier, however, he was to be disappointed. Daladier merely said that he was absolutely in accord with the statement, but that he had no further comment about it. In fact, he should have seized the opportunity to formalize the guarantee in a treaty, supplemented by immediately initiating military staff negotiations. Instead, his attitude softened noticeably. He told Chamberlain that "speaking frankly, he did not feel that he had expressed himself well on the previous evening." Then, he repeated France's determination to stand by the Czechs.[54] As Chamberlain told the cabinet afterward, "there was still one last opportunity for negotiation, but if that failed, France and Britain stood together."[55] Although he had failed to press the advantage, Daladier apparently had won an important victory for a united resistance.

It proved to be a hollow victory, however, for the British commitment was never implemented. Wilson bungled his mission miserably, failing to give his warning to Hitler until after the latter's violent Sportpalast diatribe of 26 September, by which time it was too late to have the desired sobering effect. Indeed, the enraged Hitler advanced the deadline for Czech compliance to two o'clock on the afternoon of the twenty-eighth. During the intervening period, in a bit of frantic negotiating, the French, British, and Italians, all face to face with their obligations, scrambled in disarray to head off the impending German invasion and consequent war. At this point, Bonnet reemerged from the shadows to assert himself. He appeared distraught over the fact that since they had conceded to the basic German demands, all they would be fighting over would be the form of the takeover. In a council of ministers meeting on the morning of 27 September, he declared: "It is impossible to make war. I am against general mobilization. At any price we must make a deal." The question of his resignation arose again, an act that would have undoubtedly precipitated a ministerial crisis on the very eve of the threatened German action.[56] That afternoon, the foreign minister went to see Daladier. If Bonnet is to be believed, he found the premier "shaken," and was given a blank check "to act for the best." Whether or not this actually reflected the situation is debatable.[57] Whatever the case, Bonnet took the initiative to wire Berlin at one o'clock on the morning of 28 September, to order Ambassador André François-Poncet to see Hitler and to make one last offer to assure the German government "a very large measure of satisfaction of prestige." A few hours earlier, Ambassador Phipps had alerted Bonnet to a final initiative by his government proposing a new plan for a staged occupation of Czech territory. Bonnet now gave François-Poncet orders to make certain that if the British proposal did not include an immediate occupation of the most important areas, the French were prepared to make such an offer.[58]

Clearly, Bonnet was willing to concede on every point, and just as clearly Franco–British cooperation was as deficient by the end of the crisis as it had been throughout. Moreover, the very nature of the final Bonnet initiative reflected entrenched division within the French government. This was a Bonnet initiative and not one coming from either Daladier or the ministry. In the end, even as François-Poncet urgently delivered his demarche, Hitler received Mussolini's appeal for a conference that succeeded in persuading Hitler to hold one more meeting, this time at Munich on the twenty-ninth. As René Girault has written, Hitler could easily accept the conference because "he knew perfectly henceforth the extent of the Anglo–French concessions. . . . Before Munich and on the initiatives as much French as British, the fate of the Czech problem had been settled."[59]

The story of the conference itself has been well told elsewhere. For the purposes of this study, however, it is important to note that the promise of support that Chamberlain gave to Daladier on the twenty-sixth would not have made much difference even if a solution had not been negotiated at Munich. Yet another product of Franco–British distrust was lack of cooperation in military planning. Indeed, their knowledge of each other's military capabilities and plans was woefully inadequate and might have spelled disaster if war had broken out in 1938.

Obligations to Czechoslovakia aside, an open attack on France would obviously necessitate a British response. How this would be implemented had never been worked out. Since the end of 1937, the British chiefs of staff had recognized the need for such plans, but the government had refused to permit official staff conversations for fear that they might lead to a definite commitment to France that might prejudice the attempts at appeasement by appearing provocative to Germany.[60] The French, of course, were desperate for formal staff conversations. Only late in the spring of 1938 did Britain agree to initiate army and air staff talks; naval contacts would be arranged at a later date.[61] The contacts did not begin immediately, however, and they languished during the summer months.[62] Moreover, it soon became apparent that the British had little military assistance to offer. At the end of August, Hore-Belisha bemoaned the fact that Britain could provide only two inadequately equipped divisions—a force not really strong enough to have any decisive effect.[63] It is a fact that when the September crisis began to heat up, Britain and France had no combined strategic plan nor even a general knowledge of either each other's military strategy or capacity. As Sir John Slessor, deputy director of the air staff, later put it, "It is horrifying to recall the extent of our ignorance about the military policy and forces of the nation to whom by 1938 we were morally and practically . . . committed."[64]

Given this situation, not only was it imperative that Britain give France a clear commitment of support in the event of war, but it was also vital that the two general staffs be given permission to work on a combined strategic plan that would, if necessary, make effective military cooperation possible. For this reason, the Anglo–French meeting of 25–26 September was critical from both military and diplomatic standpoints.[65] As we have already seen, during a cross-examination conducted by Simon and Chamberlain on the first day of the conference, Daladier had made a forceful, if somewhat general, statement about the condition and plans of the French armed forces. He had admitted that, although the equipment of the French air force was inferior to Germany's, its personnel was well trained.[66] Because there were many technical questions to be answered, it had been decided to send for General Gamelin, who arrived early the following day. He, too, proved to be much more optimistic than the British had anticipated—indeed, many in London had become convinced of France's poor military condition and disinclination to fight.[67] In a report that contradicted in every way the ambivalent estimates he had been issuing all spring and summer, Gamelin recognized that France would probably suffer heavily from air attacks. But he indicated that it would be able to take offensive action, particularly against the German industrial districts along the frontier. Moreover, the Siegfried Line was far from completed and only lightly defended by eight German divisions, across from which France had twenty-three divisions. If nothing else, France would at least be able to draw German troops away from an attack against Czechoslovakia. He held a high opinion of Czech military capabilities. The implicit sine qua non of success in all of this, however, would be British military support, particularly air power. As Gamelin concluded, it was *"indispensable that the French government and high command know without delay what would be . . . the possibilities of sending to France important British forces."* France could hold its own in a war, but *"in order to win the war, it will need to be helped"* (italics in original).[68] In fact, Gamelin's report represented a large exercise in bluff and deception that was, as one scholar has argued, "a deliberate attempt to stiffen the British position."[69] As a political ploy, however, it appeared to have the desired affect. As Cadogan noted in his diary the next day, all of this "seems to have put heart into the Prime Minister."[70] Indeed, it was after this meeting with Gamelin that Chamberlain gave his eleventh-hour guarantee of support to Daladier.

Yet, the French received only half a loaf. Although Hoare assumed that Chamberlain had given Daladier the specific pledge of a British expeditionary force in case of war with Germany,[71] this was not so. Moreover, there is no indication that any extensive Franco–British staff talks were subsequently approved. In fact, upon their return to Paris on the twenty-sixth, the French sent off a note to London asking "point blank" whether England would be prepared to mobilize simultaneously with them, introduce conscription, and pool their economic and financial resources.[72] Halifax, however, still pursued his diplomatic gymnastics, maintaining his distance while simultaneously trying to keep a rein on the French by persuading Bonnet to agree that "any offensive action taken by either of us henceforth . . . shall be taken only after previous consultation and agreement." Only on the evening of the twenty-eighth, well after the stage had been set for the Munich Conference, did Halifax reply to the French enquiry, emphasizing the need for concerted action and indicating that the fleet had been mobilized as had the auxiliary units of the air force.[73] This delay may have been satisfying to Bonnet, but it could not have encouraged those who wished to continue to resist German pressure. It probably made no difference; the die had been cast. Just as distrust had prevented any serious exchange of views on the diplomatic plane until very late in the game, it had also made it impossible to develop meaningful combined military plans.

An important question that often arises is why Daladier, after apparently extracting a firm British commitment to France, went to Munich and helped to negotiate away Czech independence. Was his show of strength merely for the record, as some have contended?[74] Did he intend throughout to surrender while creating the appearance that he was forced by British pressure to capitulate against his will? The British, judging from the Nichols memorandum, obviously feared such a possibility. Yet, there is little evidence to support this claim. Instead, it is more logical to seek the reasons for his behavior in his psychological makeup: Daladier's alternating acts of strength and weakness merely reflected the ambivalence of the man. It was a pattern of behavior that the "Bull of the Vaucluse" had followed throughout his career.[75] In his negotiations with the British during the Czechoslovak crisis, he merely followed a well-established pattern. He consistently entered the negotiations with firm resolve, only to yield in the end.

Admittedly, there was much on which Daladier's ambivalence could feed. He was torn by the fact that he had never really been an enthusiastic supporter of the Versailles settlement, and, as a former infantryman who had stuck it out through the horrors of the Great War, it was difficult for him to rationalize a butchery of French youth for the sake of Czechoslovakia. He also understood better than others that it was not only Czechoslovakia that was at stake—Hitler wished to dominate all of Europe. Yet, as he confided to American ambassador William C. Bullitt, while France would win a war with Germany, the only true winners would be the Bolsheviks. "The Cossacks," he said, "will rule Europe."[76] Even his commitment, often stated in public, to aid Czechoslovakia if Germany launched an invasion was never supported by a clear statement that Germany's demands were nonnegotiable. This left considerable room for doubt in all quarters about the true policy of his government.

Apart from Daladier's personal dilemma, he encountered a multitude of other problems: his government teetered on the edge of disintegration, divided between those who wanted peace at any price and those who would resist at any price; the French nation similarly battled itself, with the vocal pacifist element apparently holding the upper hand; the defeatist statements and activities of Bonnet and the one-sided reports of Phipps undermined his negotiating position; and, most important, France's apparently deplorable military situation weighed heavily on his mind.

As he flew in and out of Paris in the course of his September travels, Daladier must have looked down upon the thousands of small French homes and tree-lined boulevards and realized that it would be impossible for the pathetic French air force to prevent the widely predicted massive aerial bombardment and destruction of it all. Would a war on behalf of the Czechs be worth the price? The French estimates of comparative air power in 1938 were truly frightening. Guy La Chambre, air minister, warned Daladier that "a time might come when the number of French planes would be altogether negligible." La Chambre estimated that the French would have 600 planes (fighters and bombers) in addition to 120 British light bombers. Against these, the Germans could deploy 6,500 modern aircraft and the Italians 2,000 of mixed quality. La Chambre predicted that the Germans would "be able to bomb Paris at will."[77] General Vuillemin, commander in chief of the air staff, had visited Germany in August and had become equally alarmed, declaring to André François-Poncet, the French ambassador in Berlin, that if war broke out, "there will not be a single French plane left within fifteen days."[78] Even if French estimates of German aircraft were greatly exaggerated (which they undoubtedly were), such assessments of their relative air power intensified Daladier's predicament. As Canadian historian Robert Young has determined, the information reaching Daladier concerning French preparedness and the chances for success in a war against Germany was uniformly pessimistic: "At no time did a genuine assurance of victory come from the French high command." The situation was not nearly so dire, but Daladier had to base his actions on the information available to him.[79] Ironically, no French premier during the interwar period was as well-versed on defense policy and capabilities as was Daladier. He had been defense minister for two years and still held that portfolio in his own government. He should have been more thoroughly versed concerning the French military situation. Nevertheless, even had he known the situation, an absolutely essential element in his own mind, as well as in that of the high command, was that France needed the support of Britain.

These combined factors created a serious dilemma for Daladier. To say that his final surrender was a matter of cold, calculated duplicity designed to throw the responsibility on the British is to give him more credit for long-range planning than he deserves—not that he was incapable of duplicity and intrigue. No, his ambivalent policy truly reflected his own uncertainties. Perhaps René Girault's assessment of the man sums him up the best: Daladier "excelled in declarations of principle." He had a gift for conveying effective images that reflected the basic soundness of his judgments—for example, his comment that "the fascist government regards France like a rich uncle who takes too long to die." When confronted with haggling over policy and translating principle into concrete solution, however, he became ineffective. Too often, at that point he let himself be influenced by others. In the case of the Czech crisis, he "let himself be manipulated by his British partners who were very talented at concealing their . . . passivity under the appearance of practicality."[80] Certainly, his remark to Ambassador Bullitt upon his return from Munich reflected his sense of reality. He told the American diplomat that he did not believe Hitler's professions to be of peaceful intent. In fact, he indicated that "Chamberlain was an admirable old gentleman, like a high-minded Quaker who had fallen among bandits." The prime minister's final conversations with Hitler had not been helpful, and Daladier predicted that within six months Britain and France would be confronted with new German demands.[81] Offsetting this, however, was his feeble lament to Gamelin, "It wasn't brilliant, but I did what I could."[82]

"With an 'if,' one could put Paris in a bottle," goes an old French saying. If Daladier had only stood by Czechoslovakia. If France had taken on Germany in 1938. The possibilities are endless. In fact, however, any successful war against Germany depended, at the very least, upon firm Franco–British trust and cooperation. Yet, the evidence indicates that such a relationship did not exist during the Czech crisis of September 1938 any more than it would in 1939–40. Indeed, the mutual distrust and lack of cooperation between the two allies meant that the result would not have differed appreciably from that of 1940. In the end, any French offensive would have been a mere gesture as a prelude to camping down behind the Maginot Line, and Czechoslovakia would have gone down anyway.[83] Moreover, the lack of meaningful staff conversation meant that even if a British expeditionary force worthy of the name had existed, it would have been difficult to initiate any combined operations in time to prevent the eventual destruction of a large area of France. Indeed, if fighting had commenced in 1938, one can only imagine the number of times that painful encounters would have broken out between the French and British similar to those that occurred in 1940. Such scenes, General Weygand later recalled, were the result of "twenty years of mutual suspicion and hesitation."[84]

At no time was this interwar suspicion and hesitation more apparent than during the Czechoslovak crisis. Ambassador Bullitt thought that they had "acted like little boys doing dirty things behind the barn."[85] But both were quite conscious of the possibility of being caught and eagerly sought to direct the situation to their liking while avoiding responsibility for doing so. On the British side, the Nichols memorandum merely reflected the thoughts of a great many who, similar to Hore-Belisha, feared having "to dispute with France as to which of us really let the Czech democracy down."[86] But this was balanced by others including Sir Ivone Kirkpatrick at the British embassy in Berlin, who believed that "the French were against fighting and would not hesitate to take the first opportunity of blaming us for having dragged them into war."[87] Either way, whether in peace or war, recriminations appeared likely. To prevent this, British policy, which Halifax had hoped would keep Germany "guessing,"[88] was instead far more successful at keeping France in the dark. But the lack of consistent and meaningful consultation with the French kept them uncertain and distrustful of British plans and objectives.

For their part, the French believed that Britain was intent on placing the responsibility for surrendering Czechoslovakia on France—the tactics of Chamberlain and Halifax were proof. They feared, however, being maneuvered into a position where they would have to face a resurgent Germany alone if they stood firm. For this reason, they consistently sought the very thing Britain was fearful of giving—a firm commitment of diplomatic and military support. Such a guarantee had been the long-term goal of French policy makers throughout the 1930s. It followed, therefore, that it might be necessary to take the British lead in the short-term in such crises as the one over Czechoslovakia. Sooner or later, Britain would be forced to recognize that its own fate, as well as that of the continental states, could be secured only by the establishment of Franco–British solidarity. The fact is, however, that France could have placed itself in the driver's seat in its quest for British support. As Orme Sargent, assistant undersecretary at the Foreign Office, noted, the condition of British armaments meant that Britain was tied to France's "apron strings."[89] Yet, the French never fully seemed to grasp the fact that had they led, as Daladier gave halting indications of doing, Britain would have been forced to follow.

In the end, each side craftily maneuvered to ascertain and influence the other's position, while at the same time revealing as little as possible about its own plans and commitments. In so doing, they managed to make a difficult situation nearly impossible. This was the result, however, of years of mistrust, animosity, and even disdain. The French remained suspicious that perfidious Albion would be quite willing to "fight to the last French soldier," while Noel Coward's popular 1930s musical play, "Conversation Piece," summed up the thinking of many British. The lyrics of one song went, "Every wise and thoroughly worldly wench/Knows there's something fishy about the French!" The refrain went on, "Oh, there's always something fishy about the French!"[90] Indeed, as Bullitt lamented at the time, the world was certainly in a very sad mess.

NOTES

1. Foreign Office Memorandum, 28 September 1938, Unpublished Foreign Office Papers, file 371, vol. 21592, no. 11450/13/17. Hereafter cited as UBFO 371.
2. Henri Dutailly, *Les Problèmes de l'armée de terre française (1935–1939)* (Paris, 1988), 18–19.

3. For discussions of the issue of Soviet aid, see Anthony Adamthwaite, *France and the Coming of the Second World War* (London, 1977), 235–38; Dutailly, *Les Problèmes de l'armée de terre française*, 44–45. The most recent study of the Soviet side is Jiří Hochman, *The Soviet Union and the Failure of Collective Security, 1934–1938* (Ithaca, 1984). See also, F. Vnuk, "Munich and the Soviet Union," *Journal of Central European Affairs* 21 (October 1961): 284–304. For the French failure to give teeth to the Franco–Soviet pact by negotiating a military convention, see John E. Dreifort, "The French Popular Front and the Franco–Soviet Pact, 1936–37: A Dilemma in Foreign Policy," *Journal of Contemporary History* 6 (July 1971): 217–36.

4. For a recent study of Franco–Italian relations, see William I. Shorrock, *From Ally to Enemy: The Enigma of Fascist Italy in French Diplomacy* (Kent, Ohio, 1988). For the American position during the crisis, see John McVickar Haight, Jr., "France, the United States, and the Munich Crisis," *Journal of Modern History* 32 (December 1960): 340–58.

5. For a discussion of the nature of the *Documents diplomatiques français, 1932–1939*, as well as the problems confronting the editors of the project, see F. Gadrat and P. Renouvin, "Les Documents diplomatiques français, 1932–1939," *Revue d'histoire de la deuxième guerre mondiale* 71 (July 1968): 1–11. The memoirs and diaries of several of those who were intimately involved in the events of the period have been published. For example, see those of Sir Alexander Cadogan, *The Diaries of Sir Alexander Cadogan, 1938–1945*, ed. David Dilks (London, 1971); Oliver Harvey, *The Diplomatic Diaries of Oliver Harvey, 1937–1940*, ed. John Harvey (London, 1970); William C. Bullitt, *For the President: Personal and Secret*, ed. Orville H. Bullitt (Boston, 1972). Bullitt's correspondence is particularly valuable for the insight it gives about the concerns and activities of French statesmen. Daladier confessed that he was "very intimate" with Bullitt (Daladier's testimony, *Les Evénements survenus en France de 1933 à 1945: Témoignages et documents recueillis par la Commission d'Enquête* [Paris, 1947], I: 33, hereafter cited as *Les Evénements*). Bullitt's dispatches are doubly important because many of the French statesmen most directly involved in the crisis, such as Alexis Léger, secretary general at the Quai d'Orsay; René Massigli, deputy director of political affairs at the Quai d'Orsay; and Charles Corbin, the French ambassador in London, all have chosen, for various reasons, not to write their *souvenirs* for that period. Personal interviews with M. Charles Corbin and M. René Massigli, Paris, 7 July and 25 August 1969. For an analysis of the earlier memoirs by other French participants, including Georges Bonnet, General Maurice Gamelin, André François-Poncet, and Jean Zay, among others, see Maurice Baumont, "French Critics and Apologists Debate Munich," *Foreign Affairs* 25 (July 1947): 685–90.

6. For standard accounts of the crisis, see Telford Taylor, *Munich: The Price of Peace* (New York, 1979); Sir John Wheeler-Bennett, *Munich: Prologue to Tragedy*, 2d ed. (New York, 1963); Keith Eubank, *Munich* (Norman, Okla., 1963); Henri Noguères, *Munich: Peace for Our Time* (New York, 1965). More recent works that provide good coverage of selected aspects of the crisis include Jean-Baptiste Duroselle, *La Décadence (1932–1939)* (Paris, 1979); Keith Middlemas, *Diplomacy of Illusion: The British Government and Germany, 1937–1939* (London, 1972); Anthony Adamthwaite, *France and the Coming of the Second World War*; and Adamthwaite, "Reactions to the Munich Crisis," in *Troubled Neighbours: Franco–British Relations in the Twentieth Century*, ed. Neville Waites (London, 1971). For the most thorough guides to the earlier literature on the topic, see Francis L. Loewenheim, ed., *Peace or Appeasement: Hitler, Chamberlain and the Munich Crisis* (Boston, 1965); and Dwight E. Lee, *Munich: Blunder, Plot or Tragic Necessity?* (Lexington, Mass., 1970).

7. For Chamberlain's explanation of "Plan Z," as he called his proposed trip, see the minutes of the British cabinet meeting of 14 September 1938, Unpublished British Cabinet Papers, Cab. 23, vol. 95, 38(38)1, pp. 34–60. Hereafter cited as UBCab. 23.

8. For a detailed examination of Franco–East European relations for the period between the reoccupation of the Rhineland and the Austrian Anschluss, see John E. Dreifort,

The French Role 41

Yvon Delbos at the Quai d'Orsay: French Foreign Policy During the Popular Front, 1936–1938 (Lawrence, Kan., 1973).

9. "Comptes rendus des conversations franco–britanniques des 28 et 29 avril 1938," in Corbin (London) to Foreign Ministry, 29 April 1938, *Documents diplomatiques français, 1932–1939*, 2d ser., 9, no. 258, pp. 578–80. Hereafter quoted as *DDF*. Bonnet even chimed in to argue that Britain and France must not allow themselves to be caught once more by a new violation of treaties, "lest a major revision of east European frontiers occur." "France," he argued, "must respect its word and its signature" (p. 582).

10. Quoted in Gilbert Fergusson, "Munich: The French and British Roles," *International Affairs* 44 (October 1966): 654. For other indications of Daladier's support for Czechoslovakia, see his statements to the British during a meeting in London, 28– 29 April, "Record of Anglo–French Conversations, April 28–29, 1938," *Documents on British Foreign Policy, 1919–1939*, 3d ser., 1, no. 164, pp. 216–18. Hereafter cited as *DBFP*.

11. Phipps (Paris) to Halifax, 23 May 1938, *DBFP*, 3d ser., 1, no. 286, p. 357. This attitude represented a significant retreat from his position expressed the day before, when he had reaffirmed that France would "respect her treaty undertakings and provide the utmost help to Czechoslovakia if she is victim of aggression." Phipps (Paris) to Halifax, 22 May 1938, *DBFP*, 3d ser., 1, no. 26, p. 340. Oliver Harvey, Lord Halifax's personal secretary, noted after the crisis had passed, "The French have made it absolutely clear that they will support any course which will avoid for them the dreadful dilemma of fighting or dishonoring their signature." *Diplomatic Diaries*, 145.

12. Note du Ministre des Affaires étrangères, 20 July 1938, *DDF*, 2d ser., 10, no. 238, p. 437. Bonnet's statement shocked Beneš, whom Lacroix found in "a kind of collapse." Lacroix (Prague) to Bonnet, 21 July 1938, *DDF*, 2d ser., 10, no. 242, p. 445.

13. See Halifax's review of British obligations in the Enclosure in Halifax to Phipps (Paris), 22 March 1938, *DBFP*, 3d ser., 1, no. 106, pp. 83–86.

14. Halifax to Representatives in Berlin, Paris, Washington, Prague, and Budapest, 24 March 1938, *DBFP*, 3d ser., 1, no. 114, p. 97. Chamberlain made the statement in the course of a speech to Parliament.

15. Duroselle, *La Décadence*, 340–43; and "Compte rendu de la liaison hebdomadaire," 3 August 1938, *DDF*, 2d ser., 10, no. 325, p. 591.

16. Phipps (Paris) to Halifax, 8 September 1938, *DBFP*, 3d ser., 2, no. 807, p. 269.

17. UBCab. 23, vol. 95, 38(38)1, p. 37. Phipps had found Daladier "a very different person" from what he had been earlier in the month. Although Bonnet announced publicly on 4 September that "France will remain faithful to the pacts and treaties that it had concluded" (Duroselle, *La Décadence*, p. 343), Chamberlain reported to the cabinet that Phipps had described Bonnet as being in a "state of collapse" and "thoroughly cowed, and convinced that if war came the great cities of France and England would be laid in ruins." Oliver Harvey, private secretary to the British Foreign Secretary Lord Halifax, recorded that "further appeals came to us from Bonnet to save them at any price from war." *Diplomatic Diaries*, 179.

18. Halifax to Phipps (Paris), 12 September 1938, *DBFP*, 3d ser., 2, no. 843, p. 303.

19. Ibid. Duroselle argues that Bonnet was, in fact, most upset by a statement made by Chamberlain on 12 September, when the prime minister stated to the press that "England has no engagements in Central Europe or vis-à-vis Czechoslovakia, but that it could not remain apart from a general conflict in Europe." This was the furthest that the British had ever gone in indicating a willingness to intervene in a war, and Bonnet quickly sought to neutralize its effect by arguing that public opinion in neither country would support a war that promised to be lopsided. Note du Ministre, 13 September 1938, *DDF*, 2d ser., 11, no. 125, pp. 198–99. Nevertheless, such a British statement may have had the effect of encouraging an optimism on the part of Daladier. *La Décadence*, 344.

20. For a summary of this meeting, see Adamthwaite, *France and the Coming of the Second*

World War, 210. Apparently, Bonnet threatened to resign over the issue, although this is not certain. Supporters of a strong course of action were Paul Reynaud, Georges Mandel, Auguste Champtier de Ribes, and César Campinchi. The Bonnet position found support from Camille Chautemps, Anatole de Monzie, and Charles Pomaret. See ed. note on Lacroix (Prague) to Bonnet, 15 September 1938, *DDF*, 2d ser., 11, no. 150, p. 195.

21. Daladier to Chamberlain, 13 September 1938, *DDF*, 2d ser., 11, no. 122, p. 195.
22. Note du Ministre, 13 September 1938, *DDF*, 2d ser., 11, no. 125, p. 199. It has been suggested that Bonnet's latest fright had been encouraged by recent reports concerning the overwhelming superiority of the German air force. These reports were related by Charles Lindbergh, who had stopped off in Paris after a visit to Germany. See attached note to Bonnet's memorandum. On 14 September, Phipps reported that Bonnet had said that France would accept any solution that would avoid war. "We cannot sacrifice ten million men in order to prevent three and a half million Sudetens joining the Reich. . . . We are not ready for war and we must therefore make the most far-reaching concessions to the Sudetens and to Germany." Phipps (Paris) to Halifax, 14 September 1938, *DBFP*, 3d ser., 2, no. 874, p. 323.
23. Communication téléphonique, 14 September 1938, *DDF*, 2d ser., 11, no. 130, p. 208.
24. *DBFP*, 3d ser., 2, nos. 875, 883, pp. 323–24, 329; and Corbin (London) to Bonnet, 14 September 1938, *DDF*, 2d ser., 11, no. 133, pp. 210–11. Apparently, the French received official notice barely before it was announced to the press. Indeed, they had even less advance warning than the Americans. See Nancy H. Hooker, ed., *The Moffat Papers* (Cambridge, Mass., 1956), 202. Chamberlain's initiative apparently came as a complete surprise to Bonnet, and one diplomat recorded that it surprised the whole diplomatic corps. Juliusz Łukasiewicz, *Diplomat in Paris, 1936–1939*, ed. Wacław Jędrzejewicz (New York, 1970), 122. Leonard Mosley has written that Daladier immediately telephoned London to ask whether he should go along, but was told to stay home. *On Borrowed Time* (New York, 1971), 49.
25. Bonnet to Corbin (London), 15 September 1938, *DDF*, 2d ser., 11, no. 52, p. 232.
26. Compte rendu, 16 September 1938, *DDF*, 2d ser., 11, no. 177, pp. 267–68.
27. Lacroix (Prague) to Bonnet, 17 September 1938, *DDF*, 2d ser., 11, no. 180, pp. 274–75.
28. The "inner group" included Chamberlain, Halifax, Sir John Simon, chancellor of the exchequer, Sir Samuel Hoare, home secretary, and Sir Horace Wilson, Chamberlain's personal adviser. Halifax, Simon, and Hoare had all served as foreign secretaries. This group was frequently joined, during the Czech crisis, by Cadogan, Robert Vansittart, and William Strang from the Foreign Office.
29. Quoted in Middlemas, *Diplomacy of Illusion*, 347. This attitude reflected a rather popular belief of the time that France could not hold a government for longer than six months nor a secret for more than half an hour. The group proceeded to explore the possibility of presenting France with a fait accompli in the form of a statement by Lord Runciman that a plebiscite in the Sudetenland was the only solution to the problem. A letter from former French Minister of Foreign Affairs Pierre-Etienne Flandin was read, predicting that France would not go to war to prevent such a plebiscite. Conveniently, Flandin does not mention such a letter in his memoirs, *Politique française, 1919–1940* (Paris, 1947).
30. UBCab. 23, vol. 95, 39(38)1, p. 83. Cadogan said that he went to Corbin to "tell him something—not too much!" *Diaries*, 99.
31. UBCab. 23, vol. 95, 39(38)1, p. 83. See also Phipps (Paris) to Halifax, 17 September 1938, *DBFP*, 3d ser., 2, no. 907, p. 361. Phipps asked that Bonnet be included in a meeting, because "he, more than certain other French Ministers, realizes the weakness of France." Bonnet was reported as being "somewhat incensed" that France had not been taken into consultation immediately upon Chamberlain's return. UBCab. 23, vol. 95, 39(38)1, p. 86.
32. UBCab. 23, vol. 95, 39(38)1, p. 83.

33. Ibid., pp. 88, 99. Only two cabinet ministers, Oliver Stanley and Duff Cooper, objected to this approach. As Cooper put it, Britain was "in danger of being accused of truckling to Dictators, and of offending our best friends" (p. 106).

34. In addition to Daladier and Bonnet, the French delegation included Charles Corbin (French ambassador in London), Alexis Léger (secretary general of the foreign ministry), Charles Rochet (deputy director of European affairs), Jules Henry (Bonnet's chef de cabinet), and Roland de Margerie (secretary at the French embassy in London).

35. For descriptions of the 18 September meeting, see Chamberlain's account to the cabinet on the following day in UBCab. 23, vol. 95, 40(38)2; "Record of Anglo–French Conversations of September 18, 1938," DBFP, 3d ser., 2, no. 928, pp. 373–400; and Compte rendu des conversations franco–britannique du 18 septembre 1938, DDF, 2d ser., 2, no. 212, pp. 309–33.

36. Cadogan, Diaries, 100.

37. Ibid. Cadogan made a point of noting in his diary, "independence (not integrity!)."

38. R. J. Minney, ed., The Private Papers of Hore-Belisha (London, 1960), 142.

39. UBCab. 23, vol. 95, 40(38)2, p. 131.

40. René Girault, "La décision gouvernementale en politique extérieure," in Edouard Daladier, Chef de Gouvernement, ed. René Rémond and Janine Bourdin (Paris, 1977), 216.

41. Ibid., 134. The irony of the situation is that, according to Léon Noël, the French ambassador in Warsaw (how authoritative he could be from such a distance must be questioned), it had been precisely Bonnet's plan to pin on Britain the responsibility for abandoning Czechoslovakia. "But the British did not allow themselves to be caught in this maneuver." L'Agression allemande contre la Pologne (Paris, 1946), 202.

42. For a good summary of the council debate, see Duroselle, La Décadence, 347–48. Bonnet again reiterated that the Czechs knew that France would not intervene without Britain. Daladier pointed out that it would be impossible to aid the Czechs.

43. Comptes rendus d'un entretien de M. Georges Bonnet avec M. Osušky, 19 September 1938, DDF, 2d ser., 11, no. 222, pp. 347–48.

44. Halifax still wanted to maintain some distance from the French. He thought that it might appear as though Britain were initiating some "sinister plot" to increase pressure on Czechoslovakia by inviting the French back to London so soon. UBCab. 23, vol. 95, 42(38)1, p. 182.

45. See Duroselle, La Décadence, 352. For Daladier's account, see Les Evénements, 1, 34. General Gamelin indicated that Daladier had confided that he was having difficulties in his ministry, and that Bonnet had threatened to resign. General Maurice Gamelin, Servir, 2: Le Prologue du drame, 1930–août 1939 (Paris, 1946), 350. Bonnet, in his memoirs, does not indicate that he had planned to resign and reiterates that the decision was unanimous. Défense de la paix, 2: 267. See also Jean Zay, Carnets secrets de Jean Zay (Paris, 1942), 11–17; and UBFO 371, vol. 21744, no. 11264/1941/18.

46. UBCab. 23, vol. 95, 43(38)1, pp. 226–27.

47. Lord Strang, Home and Abroad (London, 1956), 140.

48. The following day Gamelin gave his military appraisal, which basically agreed with Daladier's analysis.

49. For a report concerning the meetings of 25–26 September, see Chamberlain's account and the cabinet discussion in UBCab. 23, vol. 95, 44(38)1, pp. 235–44; and UBCab. 23, vol. 95, 45(38)1, pp. 247–49. No full account of the meeting exists in the published British documents. The complete record of the conference, however, can be found in the unpublished Foreign Office records. See "Visit of French Ministers to London, September 25–26, 1938," UBFO 371, vol. 21733, no. 11264/1941/18. The French record can be found in DDF, 2d ser., 11, nos. 356, 375, 376, pp. 537–48, 565–74.

50. Middlemas, Diplomacy of Illusion, 385.

51. Hore-Belisha recorded that as he passed Daladier at the end of the session, he said

"courage," and Daladier responded, "Il faut tenir." Minney, *Private Papers of Hore-Belisha*, 147.

52. See UBCab. 23, vol. 95, 43–45(38), for the increasing restlessness of the cabinet, as Cooper and Stanley were now joined by others, including Viscount Hailsham and Earl Winterton. Even Halifax admitted that he had "found his opinion changing somewhat in the last day or so" (p. 198). See also Minney, *Private Papers of Hore-Belisha*, 147; and Harvey, *Diplomatic Diaries*, 187–98.

53. UBCab. 23, vol. 95, 45(38)1, p. 248.

54. Ibid., 248–49.

55. Ibid., 249. To Duff Cooper, probably as well as others, this change in Chamberlain's policy seemed like a "complete reversal," *Old Men Forget*, 237.

56. See Note du Ministre, 27 September 1938, *DDF*, 2d ser., 11, no. 400, pp. 605–6. Bonnet apparently told Jules Henry, the director of his staff, that within two days he would no longer be foreign minister.

57. *For the President*, 290.

58. Bonnet to François-Poncet (Berlin), 28 September 1938, *DDF*, 2d ser., 11, no. 413, pp. 629–30.

59. Girault, "La décision gouvernementale en politique extérieure": 218.

60. Sir John Slessor, *Central Blue: The Autobiography of Sir John Slessor, Marshal of the RAF* (New York, 1957), 147; and Sir Henry Pownall, *Chief of Staff: The Diaries of Lieutenant-General Sir Henry Pownall*, ed. Brian Bond (Hamden, Conn., 1973), 164. For a study of Franco–British military considerations during the crisis, see Derrik B. Adams, "The Role of Military Considerations in Anglo–French Decision-Making in the Munich Crisis" (Ph.D. dissertation, University of Denver, 1970). General Sir Edmund Ironsides, chief of the Imperial General Staff, noted: "The Cabinet, in a muddled kind of way, are terrified of making an Expeditionary Force.... I don't blame them.... Once we are landed, our commitment is limitless.... [The French] only wish to get us committed, and we are then harnessed to the cart driven by them." Sir Edmund Ironsides, *Time Unguarded: The Ironsides Diaries, 1937–1940* (New York, 1962), 42.

61. Record of Anglo–French Conversations, 28–29 April, 1938, *DBFP*, 3d ser., 1, no. 164, pp. 199–222. See also Pownall, *Chief of Staff*, 144.

62. For example, Colonel F.G. Beaumont-Nesbitt, the British military attaché in Paris, did not receive his instructions for opening the discussions with the French General Staff until a month later. Pownall, *Chief of Staff*, 149.

63. Minney, *Private Papers of Hore-Belisha*, 138.

64. Slessor, *Central Blue*, 146. Moreover, Slessor indicates that the information that filtered through concerning the French equipment was disturbing. For example, when Charles Lindbergh stopped off in London after visiting Germany and France, frightening the latter with his reports of German air superiority, he told the British that "the stuff [the French] are now flying is so obsolete it should have been burnt ten years ago" (p. 222). For more on the status of Franco–British military cooperation, see Adamthwaite, *France and the Coming of the Second World War*, 226–31.

65. As the crisis developed in early September, the French took their first military measures by calling up selected reservists and bringing their formations along the German frontier up to full strength. When the Godesberg terms became known they took the wraps off the Czechs and began to speed up their own mobilization. For an account of the French military activities during the crisis, see Gamelin, *Servir*, 2, 344–50; and Colonel van Cutsen (War Office) to Strand (Foreign Office), 12 September 1938, UBFO 371, vol. 2111596, no. 9877/36/17. The British moved ever so slowly, merely implementing "precautionary steps" in preparation for mobilization. Permission to call up antiaircraft personnel had been delayed, and, despite the pleas of Duff Cooper, mobilization of the fleet had been postponed. See Cooper's account of his efforts in *Old Men Forget*, 227–40.

66. UBCab. 23, vol. 95, 44(38)1, p. 237. Chamberlain considered Daladier's answers to be evasive (p. 238).

67. The French attitude must have been shocking to the British, for Phipps's telegrams, based largely on talks with Bonnet, had become uniformly defeatist. See also, for example, Cadogan, *Diaries*, 103, and Secretary of Air Kingsley Wood's analysis of the situation prior to the French arrival. UBCab. 23, vol. 95, 43(38)1, p. 205.
68. Compte rendu des conversations techniques de Général Gamelin au Cabinet Office, 26 September 1938, *DDF*, 2d ser., 11, no. 376, pp. 569–75. UBCab. 23, vol. 95, 45(38)Appendix, pp. 258–59. This document was classified as a "most secret" statement made by Chamberlain to the cabinet concerning his meeting with Gamelin. For Gamelin's account, see *Servir*, 2, 350–54. It could not have helped his frame of mind to find the British "feeling that they were not ready for action" (p. 350). Nevertheless, he left the impression with Inskip that "French dispositions would be made independently of any British assistance by air or land." UBCab. 23, vol. 95, 45(38)2, p. 249.
69. Young, "French Policy and the Munich Crisis," 195.
70. Cadogan, *Diaries*, 106. How much Gamelin impressed the British military is debatable. Slessor thought that the French plans were "optimistic to the point of lunacy." *Central Blue*, 149. Ironsides believed that an offensive against Germany was something that France "could not sustain for a minute." *Ironsides Diaries*, 29. Pownall thought the French plan merely amounted to an advance to the Siegfried Line and then a withdrawal to the Maginot Line. *Chief of Staff*, 163.
71. Viscount Templewood, *Nine Troubled Years* (London, 1954), 314.
72. Phipps (Paris) to Halifax, 26 September 1938, *DBFP*, 3d ser., 2, no. 1120, p. 558; and Pownall, *Chief of Staff*, 163.
73. Halifax to Phipps (Paris), 28 September 1938, *DBFP*, 3d ser., 2, no. 1191, p. 602. Halifax to Phipps (Paris), 27 September 1938, *DBFP*, 3d ser., 2, no. 1150, p. 582.
74. See Adamthwaite, "Reactions to the Munich Crisis": 183.
75. Witness his behavior, for example, during the riots of 4 February 1936, or as minister of war during the entire debate concerning nonintervention during the Spanish Civil War, when it was nearly impossible to determine his stance.
76. Bullitt, *For the President*, 293.
77. Bullitt to secretary of state, 28 September 1938, President's Secretary File: France, Bullitt folder, Franklin D. Roosevelt Library, Hyde Park, New York. Hereafter cited as PSF: France (Bullitt). This report of La Chambre's estimate of French air power has been subsequently published in Bullitt, *For the President*, 297–99. The frightened La Chambre had already sent his family to Brittany.
78. André François-Poncet, *Souvenirs d'une ambassade à Berlin* (Paris, 1946), 326. Vuillemin to La Chambre, 26 September 1938, *DDF*, 2d ser., 11, no. 377, pp. 575–77. Vuillemin's gloomy and pessimistic reports, which did not take into account potential Czech or Soviet air forces, were widely distributed in government circles and must have had a significant influence on the discussion and thinking of the leadership. See Adamthwaite, *France and the Coming of the Second World War*, 238–40. See also Noël, *L'Agression allemande*, 224, for his estimate of French weakness.
79. Young, "French Policy and the Munich Crisis"; and Adamthwaite, *France and the Coming of the Second World War*, 232. Daladier told Bullitt later: "If I had a thousand bombers behind me to support the voice of France, I would have been in a much stronger position at Munich to resist Hitler's demands." Quoted in Young: 204.
80. Girault, "La décision gouvernementale en politique extérieure," 222.
81. Bullitt (Paris) to secretary of state, 3 October 1938, *FRUS, 1938*, I: 711–12.
82. Quoted in Jean-Pierre Azéma, *From Munich to Liberation, 1938–1944* (London, 1984), 9.
83. General Requin, in whose sector such an offensive would have been launched, prophesied to Bullitt: "It means the end of a race." Bullitt to secretary of state, 13 June 1938, PSF: France (Bullitt).
84. Quoted by John C. Cairns, "The Collapse Was European," in *The Fall of France, 1940: Causes and Responsibility*, 2d ed., ed. Samuel M. Osgood (Lexington, Mass., 1972), 96.
85. Bullitt to Roosevelt, 20 September 1938, PSF: France (Bullitt).
86. Minney, *Private Papers of Hore-Belisha*, 141.

87. Ivone Kirkpatrick, *The Inner Circle* (London, 1959), 133.
88. UBCab. 23, vol. 94, 35(38)1, p. 292.
89. See Sargent's minutes of 12 October 1938 attached to UBFO 371, vol. 4799, no. 12161/1050/17. See also Slessor, *Central Blue*, 147.
90. Noel Coward, "Conversation Piece," in *The Collected Plays of Noel Coward: Play Parade* (London, 1939), vol. 2, 366.

3

The Czechoslovak View

Joseph Frederick Zacek

The "Munich Question" is a rich complex of issues—at once both broad and narrow, political and ethical, historical and contemporary—of worldwide applicability and of specifically Czechoslovak significance. For the world, "Munich" is a familiar synonym for diplomatic betrayal and the appeasement of aggressors. For the Czechs, the term "Mnichované" (Munichites) and "Mnichovanství" (Munichism) are no less pejorative. The difference is that, despite the vast amount of literature on the subject, Czechoslovak writings and viewpoints (beyond a few obvious ones) are not widely known outside that country. From the Munich Conference to the present day, the Czech side of the debate—for political or linguistic reasons—has been comparatively inaccessible to, and ignored by, the rest of the world.

The Czechs, however, have been doing an immense amount of talking about "Munich" among themselves. No segment of Czech society since 1938 has been able either to escape the "Munich Trauma" or to resist the compulsion to examine and reexamine the subject endlessly. "Munich," writes Jan Křen, "is one of those great, dark questions of our history to which one must constantly return."[1] President Edvard Beneš, his close political collaborators, the socioeconomic stratum they represented, the communists who replaced them in 1948, and the Czech people as a whole—those who lived through Munich and its aftermath, as well as those born since who have some embarrassing questions for their elders—all have been preoccupied with the Munich question and have developed their own explanation for it and for their own role in it.

Beneš has stated that, during the last ten years of his life, Munich was his idée fixe. Whether he had made the correct decision during the terrible crisis and the way in which posterity would judge him for it were questions that plagued him. He rarely failed to refer to Munich in any significant publication or public utterance, and the complete political and moral negation of it became "the single goal of his life." The final rationale and personal self-justification he worked out during the war were not published until 1968. But long before then, during World War II, his close collaborators, Táborský, Smutný, Opočenský, Feierabend, and Ripka ("those whose hands had prepared the Munich betrayal"),[2] had made the basic scenario public.[3] Fundamentally, they insist on the inescapability of Czechoslovakia's capitulation, and place the blame for it squarely on the governments of its allies—France and Britain. Numerous factors forced Prague to choose between capitulating to Hitler's demands and delivering the nation to his diabolical will, on the one hand, and fighting alone, committing national suicide, and plunging Europe into a war for which it was not yet prepared, on the other. Some of these factors were: Hitler's exploitation of the Sudeten Achilles' heel and the cooperation of Czechoslovakia's right-wing parties; the short-sighted, even cowardly, reluctance of the British and French governments to risk involving their own peoples in war to defend their exposed Czechoslovak ally against Germany; and the unbearable pressures these governments placed upon the Czechoslovak leadership. The Czechs, as in other crises, chose reason and sacrifice. In the end, the Czech nation and its leaders, "who suffered for everyone and harmed no one," would emerge morally justified. According to Czechoslovak communist historians, this rationale was developed to justify not only Beneš and his cohorts but the entire bourgeoisie, the class that controlled Czechoslovakia in 1938 and was collectively responsible for handing it over to Hitler. In communist eyes, Munich even betrayed the Czech middle class's own much-touted "Masarykism," the defense of humanitarian principles linked to the self-defense of the Czechoslovak nation. In their view, the "Munich Complex" will forever haunt the conscience of the Czech bourgeoisie.

"No writer," claimed a member of Beneš's wartime government-in-exile, "no historian has the power to describe the terror and the pain that went through the Czech lands after Munich."[4] The Czechs were demoralized by the loss of their national and geographic frontiers, which had remained virtually unaltered for centuries and had been regarded as indispensable to the state's defense and integral to the national tradition. Later, especially when the capitulation at Munich became linked with charges of Czech nonresistance, and even collaboration, under Nazi rule, some of the pain turned to guilt, feelings of inferiority, and a loss of national self-confidence. Perhaps this topic of investigation is more amenable to techniques of mass psychology than to traditional historical analysis. Since little can be found on it in print, one is forced to approach it obliquely, mostly through contemporary novels and poetry by such writers as Marie Majerová, František Halas, and Vítězslav

Nezval, and reminiscences of eyewitnesses.[5] That the issue continues to trouble the Czechs, however, is evident to anyone who has broached the topics of Munich or the wartime pattern of behavior with practically any adult Czech, regardless of his or her political coloration. The response is immediate, emphatic, emotional, and defensive, based on the rationale that to resist Munich would have meant national suicide—once the frontiers were lost, all further resistance was impossible, and German occupation was, therefore, inevitable. The accessibility of the Bohemian–Moravian terrain and the great size of the occupying force would have made opposition ineffectual and suicidal. In these circumstances, the Czechs' only responsibility was to save their nation.

Most of the writing about Munich published in Czechoslovakia has, of course, been produced by Marxist historians. Representing the new masters of the state since 1948, they inherited the function of analyzing and interpreting this major and controversial issue from the nation's past. They were more than eager to do it. The debacle of the previous regime, still painfully imbedded in popular memory and ripe for embellishment from the domestic archives, presented them with a classic opportunity to discredit their bourgeois enemies and bolster their own following among the masses. Their writings, which also are not well known outside Czechoslovakia,[6] follow a rough periodization: highly dogmatic, rigidly schematic, rather amateurish indictments and explanations until the mid-1950s; increasingly sophisticated analyses and conclusions based on steadily growing historiographical expertise from the mid-1950s to the early 1960s; dangerously objective interpretations, often highly critical of previous Marxist work on the subject, in the years of the Prague Spring, 1967 and 1968; and a return to the orthodox Marxist line, though possibly with greater polish and historiographical ingenuity, in "normalized" Czechoslovakia during the past two decades. Certain subordinate issues, such as the role of the Sudeten Germans,[7] the sincerity of the Soviet Union's offer of unilateral aid, the diplomatic irresponsibility of France and Britain, to be sure, have not aroused significant debate, except during the 1960s. Other issues, however, such as Beneš's personal guilt and motivation, the degree of culpability of the Czech bourgeoisie, the relative weight of domestic and foreign factors, and the role of the Czechoslovak Communist Party itself, have undergone almost continual revision.

There were few nuances in the Czechoslovak Marxist treatment of Munich in the first half of the 1950s.[8] Western politicians were uniformly condemned for having engineered the betrayal; even its notable opponents such as Churchill were unceremoniously lumped with Chamberlain and Daladier. Similarly undifferentiated was the archvillain—

the Czechoslovak bourgeoisie. Apparent disagreements within the bourgeois camp were regarded as mere tactical maneuvers aimed against the masses, who wanted to resist Hitler and were feared by the bourgeoisie. Beneš, aided by his loyal cronies of the *Hrad* (Castle) and the "reformist" political parties, was the devil-in-chief, the focal point of the "conspiracy against the masses," an open agent of the "Western imperialists," an example of "inveterate anti-Sovietism," and the mechanic of "the base betrayal of the interests of the people, the nation, the state, democracy, and peace." Czechoslovak Marxist historiography unquestionably served the ideological needs of the Party—particularly in the latter's campaign against "cosmopolitanism." Its "teachings from history" had a dissemination so massive that Western historians might well envy it. Evident inconsistencies in its slogans—for instance, with which "democratic, non-communist elements" in the country was the Czechoslovak Communist Party urging a "popular front" in 1938, if the entire bourgeoisie leaned toward fascism?—were simply dismissed. In the early 1950s, it ignored pre-1948 Marxist publications that separated the Czech bourgeois classes into a "progressive" faction (Masaryk, Beneš, the *Hrad*) who wanted to defend the Republic and a "reactionary" faction (primarily the Agrarian Party) that represented the big capitalist interests and was profascist.

From the mid-1950s, with the deepening maturity of Czech Marxist historiography and the increasing accumulation of new documentary evidence, the old, bald formulas became difficult to maintain, and a more complex explanation began to emerge.[9] It now appeared unlikely that the *Hrad* and its bourgeois constituents had consciously and secretly plotted Munich together with Hitler and the Western powers. Beneš was transformed from a demonic to a tragic figure—from a Western agent to the pathetic and intimidated leader of a small state. The Great Powers themselves now became the real villains, and Beneš, with his avowedly pro-Western orientation, their effective, though possibly unwilling, tool. Three interwar political "lines" were now accepted: the *Hrad* attempted to maintain a Czechoslovak bourgeois democracy and align its foreign policy with the West's; the "agrarian reaction" aimed to integrate Czechoslovakia with Nazi Germany; and the Communist Party strove to defend the republic with a "popular front" and the help of the Soviet Union. There were some discrepancies, however. The communists had openly supported General Syrový's government, which was embarrassing. A lame explanation was offered to the effect that, at the time, the masses still followed Beneš and could not have been swayed by communist tactics. This factor rendered the Party vulnerable to the charges of left-wing critics that it had actually been subordinate to, rather than a leader of, the masses.

In a new approach during the early 1960s, Czech Marxist historians took a new tack, embarking on broad studies of interwar European diplomacy, especially Czechoslovak foreign policy.[10] As a result, the impression of interwar Czechoslovakia was that of far more than a mere stooge of the Western powers. Czechoslovakia emerges as far more of an active political force in its own right—dedicated to developing a system of collective security for Europe, and thereby ensuring its own security. Czechoslovakia had persisted the longest in striving toward that goal; it had refused to imitate such countries as Poland, Yugoslavia, France, Romania, and Britain in seeking a direct accommodation with Hitler and adopting an official anti-Soviet stance. When the West chose appeasement, Czechoslovakia was left stranded. If Beneš had relied too long on collective security, the reason was that he had overestimated the strength of the anti-Hitler, antiappeasement forces in Britain and France. He was guilty of "exaggerated optimism," but there was, none-theless, a realistic chance until the very end that the antiappeasement forces would win—that there was a solution other than Munich to the German–Czechoslovak confrontation. Beneš's thinking also justified the support given him by the Communist Party, which, like the Soviet Union itself, aimed to ally itself with all antifascist forces in Europe. If, however, Beneš himself could not accept a common front with the com-munists and preferred to steer a course between the right and left extremes of Czechoslovak politics, it was simply because of his ingrained bourgeois-capitalist "fear of the people," his apprehension about the growing mass appeal of socialism.

This brief outline indicates the stage reached by Czechoslovak com-munist historiography in its treatment of Munich when the Prague Spring briefly freed the country's historians from the constraints of unchallenged Marxist ideology. During that short season, in 1968, two noteworthy works were published on the Munich crisis—Edvard Beneš's personal memoirs, *Mnichovské dny* (Munich days), and Míla Lvová's *Mnichov a Edvard Beneš* (Munich and Edvard Beneš). Both books remain well known to Czech historians, although, submerged by the invasion and the quick reimposition of sovietization in the autumn of 1968, neither one was extensively reviewed or mentioned either in the popular press or in scholarly publications. A French version of Beneš's memoirs published in Paris in 1969 has received very little public attention,[11] and Lvová's book, hailed in Czech intellectual circles as a model of pain-staking, imaginative historiography, is proscribed from Czechoslovakia's libraries and bookstores, and Lvová has lost her professional position.

Beneš's *Munich Days,* completed in rough draft in 1943–44, was intended as the first of three volumes of memoirs on the period since 1938. Of that series, only the second volume appeared during his lifetime, *From Munich to New War and New Victory.* An incomplete, mimeographed version of the first volume, including the Munich crisis, appeared in London in 1955;[12] the full version of it, with a valuable documentary appendix, was rushed through the press in Czechoslovakia in the record time of six months in 1968, which testified to the popular rehabilitation of the maligned president then in process. Most significant, perhaps, is that the book was published at all. It is, to be sure, the last memoir of a leading participant in the Munich proceedings to be made public, but it is not rich in revelatory new facts. It illustrates once again the cleverness of Nazi propaganda against the Czechs and the Czechs' ineptitude at countering it. It gives the details of the extremely complicated changes in governmental structure on every level—arrangements so complex that it is virtually inconceivable that any governmental business could have been conducted at all—that the Czechoslovak leaders were formally willing to concede to placate the Sudeten German minority and their own Western allies. Beneš exhibits a warm attitude toward the Soviets, although individuals close to him have insisted that this attitude had changed by 1947–48, and that his revisions of the manuscript to that effect were interrupted by his death. The chief value of this book lies elsewhere, however. Similar to the famous *Czech Black Book* that was compiled during the 1968 invasion of Czechoslovakia, it describes, step by step, the feelings of a victim who is slowly being strangled.[13] Despite Beneš's complicated legal-diplomatic-literary style, the reader cannot help but experience the crushing pressure and despair of the president. Indeed, even the redogmatized post-1968 Marxist historians in Czechoslovakia are not immune to this impression, which they cite frequently.

Míla Lvová's *Munich and Edvard Beneš* is nothing less than an attempt to reconstruct the Czechoslovak president's thinking in the fifteen days preceding, and the five days after, the Munich Conference. It amounts to a meticulously reasoned, warmly compassionate defense, if not exoneration, of Beneš. The vulgarized sketch of the early 1950s of Beneš as the puppet of the bourgeois class is completely erased and replaced by an intricate portrait that comes perilously close to the one first presented to the West by Beneš and his associates during the war. There is never any doubt in this book that Beneš consistently defended his nation's interests. He capitulated only when, in his view, no other acceptable path was open to him—when the Western powers had finally chosen to abandon collective security in favor of appeasement, and left him isolated. (Beneš had often said that it was not the commander of the Czechoslovak army, but the Czechoslovak foreign minister, who would have to guarantee the country's defense.) He was not a coward afraid to fight alone; he simply refused to risk the annihilation of his people in a hopelessly ill-matched war with Germany. It was clear that once hostilities began Czechoslovakia would have to hold out alone for a significant period, absorbing enormous punishment, particularly through air raids, while waiting—and hoping—that the European powers would intervene. Would they intervene? Most important, would they intervene in time to save the Czech and Slovak peoples from obliteration? Would the defeated anti-Munich elements in France and Britain recover their strength and reverse their governments' policies quickly enough? Beneš doubted it, and would not wager the lives of his countrymen on it. To be sure, he could have gone to war with Soviet military assistance. Lvová does not deny that Beneš feared the sovietization of Czechoslovakia nor that, more important, he feared a negative reaction from the Western powers to his acceptance of Soviet aid. But, attacking one of the holiest of Czech Marxist dogmas about Munich, she points out that no concrete documentary evidence exists to prove unequivocally that Moscow actually offered unqualified unilateral aid to the Czechs.[14] Although Moscow did make overt military preparations earlier in September, at the time of Munich, it seemed to be pulling away, probably fearful of provoking the aggression of Nazi Germany, as well as that of the Western powers, against itself. Furthermore, there is little evidence that Soviet military aid, if given, would have been effective. Lvová points out in deadpan earnest that at the very time of her writing the stationing of Soviet troops on Czechoslovak soil is being justified by the great difficulty of transporting them all the way from the Soviet Union in time to counter a potential attack from West Germany. Surely, this problem would have been just as great, if not greater, in 1938, considering the less-developed military technology available thirty years earlier. History does not take place without the participation of people, concludes Lvová, but it does sometimes take place against the best efforts of some of them, "and that includes even the second president of the First Czechoslovak Republic, Dr. Edvard Beneš."

Intellectually constrained from 1968 to 1988, Czechoslovakia produced little significant historical scholarship on Munich. The subject certainly continued to attract a respectable stream of researchers, especially in connection with conferences held in the special anniversary years, 1973, 1978, 1983, and 1988. The results, however, in terms of both the topics treated and the treatment, are very similar to the publications that appeared before the Prague Spring, though generally more detailed, thanks to the growing fund of relevant primary and secondary material.

The thirty-fifth anniversary of Munich witnessed the usual commemorative scholarly conference as well as two noteworthy events of a different sort—a controversial epic film and an international treaty. The wide-screen, technicolor documentary *Dny zrady* (Days of betrayal) arrived in Czechoslovak theaters in early 1973. Lavishly filmed in the original locations, employing masses of actors, including carefully selected look-alikes playing the central characters, and drawing its scenario and dialogues largely from historical records, the film was expected to draw huge crowds. It was widely advertised for its "topical" and "contemporary" importance and recommended especially to the younger generation, to remind it of "who alone remained at the side of Czechoslovakia" and "who alone warned unequivocally against Hitler's imperialism and the betrayal of the Czech bourgeoisie."[15] After the first days, attendance dropped off so sharply that the theaters had to be filled with brigades of government employees, transported en masse to view the film during working hours. Little wonder, for the production alternated between a lampoon and a pageant-epic of the Cecil B. DeMille variety. The villains included a yawning, foppish Chamberlain and the swinish Agrarian leader Beran, sloppily guzzling champagne. The heroes ranged from an earnest, pipe-puffing Gottwald urging the government to "go to the factories" to ranks of sober-faced Czech citizens and sadly proud Czech soldiers who "wanted to defend their country but were not allowed to." Interestingly enough, Beneš, played by the actor Jiří Pleskot, a remarkable look-alike, was treated with marked gentleness, even sympathy. This provoked the ire of the old Marxist warhorse, Václav Král, whose career had been badly shaken in 1968 but who had since recovered his earlier authority among Czechoslovak historians with a vengeance. In his review of the film,[16] Král warned that Beneš must not be considered merely a passive victim of Western pressures: he had deliberately based Czechoslovak foreign policy exclusively on Western support, had himself indicated to the French which border areas of Czechoslovakia could be ceded to Germany, and had even solicited Western diplomatic pressure at decisive moments to justify his backsliding to an alarmed Czechoslovak populace. In addition, had he not complained that during the Munich crisis virtually all of the day-to-day negotiations had been placed in his hands alone?

The following September, at an international scholarly conference on "Europe and Munich" held in Liberec (Reichenberg), the former Sudeten German stronghold, Král was able to present the official Czechoslovak Marxist post-1968 line on Munich—a line that remains basically unchanged to the present—repudiating the revisionism of the late 1960s and chastising those responsible for it. After a grandiose "review" of the world literature on the Munich question, he delivered only a dull and dogmatic reaffirmation of all of the formulas of the doctrinaire early 1950s.[17] Some of his listeners insisted that Král, an exceptionally prolific but rather unoriginal writer, must simply have dusted off something he had written twenty years earlier, inserting a few pointed warnings to the hapless Lvová and the battered, but still stubborn, survivors of the Prague Spring. He warned that a historian who doubts that a popular front could have saved the republic in 1938 does not believe in the power of the people. He pointed out that to many Czechs "even in recent years," Masaryk and Beneš had been the objects of sentimental attachment, but that they needed to be judged very critically. "To be sure," he added, "it is indispensable that this be done soberly, temperately, tactfully, and decently"—a remarkable exhortation coming from one notorious for his coarse verbal bullying of his opponents.

In December 1973, Czechoslovakia and West Germany finally signed a treaty normalizing their relations.[18] The negotiations, conducted intermittently since 1967, had repeatedly foundered over the juridical nature of the Munich Pact. The Czechoslovaks insisted that it had been "legally invalid from the start," the Germans that it was "currently invalid." (The final wording of the treaty merely declared the Pact "void in regard to [their] mutual relations under [the present] treaty.") The ghost of Edvard Beneš was present even here, providing the means for a convenient compromise. Attempting to secure recognition for his government-in-exile in wartime London as the continuation of the Czechoslovak government of 1938, Beneš had insisted that the Munich Pact had been automatically canceled by the events of 15 March 1939. Another Czech reference to Beneš almost backfired, however. In a pamphlet intended to summarize the Czechoslovak case, Král charged that the Czech president had "solicited" the Munich Pact from Hitler and the Western powers to excuse his surrender in the eyes of the Czech populace.[19] The pamphlet was hastily withdrawn from sale when Sudeten German expellee groups in West Germany, bitterly opposed to the new treaty, began to exploit Král's charges in arguing that the Munich Pact had not, in fact, been imposed upon Czechoslovakia by force.

It is discouraging to compare Czechoslovak publications on Munich over the past two decades with those that appeared before the Prague Spring. Collections of documents[20] and of essays[21] and monographs are all mired in the same time-worn issues and dusty dogmas. Much of the newer production consists of journalistic popularization,[22] trivial accounts of the contemporary repercussions of Munich across Bohemia and Moravia, and homely reminiscences of the time by members of a variety of occupational groups, such as teachers or athletes. Noticeable, although not really new, is the repeated and heavy emphasis on the fervent desire of the Czechoslovak masses to defend themselves militarily, the adequacy of the Czechoslovak forces to defend the country, and the genuineness of the Soviet offer, based on the treaty of 1935, to come to Czechoslovakia's aid.[23] Similarly noticeable and familiar is the unequivocal thesis of the only broad synthetic study of Munich to appear during this most recent period—namely, 1978—Jaroslav César's *Mnichov 1938* (Munich 1938). This thesis held that Munich was not primarily a tactical miscalculation of the Western powers, or even a moral betrayal of Czechoslovakia, but simply part of the continuing long-term war of the capitalist–imperialist camp against the Soviet Union and the international revolutionary socialist movement, in which Czechoslovakia's and its people's sacrifice to Hitler's fascism was merely incidental.

Bibliographical and substantive research for this chapter was, necessarily, terminated in early 1988. Given the stirring events in Czechoslovakia since late 1989, specifically the successful popular repudiation of communist domination and Soviet influence, we may well expect a new period of innovation and revisionism in the Czechoslovak historiography of Munich.[24] It is unlikely that Munich will ever cease to have deep significance for the Czechs. Similar to the Holocaust for the Jews, with whom the Czechs have often been compared by their historians in the past, the "Munich Betrayal" has found a permanent place in their consciousness. Speaking to the Czechs of the acknowledged zenith of their history, the complex and controversial Hussite Revolution of the fifteenth century, Zdeněk Nejedlý, the nestor of communist Czechoslovakia, once said: "Tell me what you think about Hussitism, and I will tell you who you are."[25] He could have said the same about the nadir of Czechoslovak history—Munich.

NOTES

1. Jan Křen, *Do emigrace: Buržoazní odboj, 1938–1939* (Into emigration: the bourgeois resistance, 1938–1939) (Prague, 1963), 85.
2. Ibid., 88.
3. See, for example, Hubert Ripka, *Munich, Before and After* (London, 1939); Boris Celovský, *Das Münchener Abkommen von 1938* (Stuttgart, 1958); and Otakar Odložilík, "Concerning Munich and the Ides of March," *Journal of Central European Affairs* 9, no. 4 (1949–50): 419–28.
4. Křen, *Do emigrace*, 106.

5. See, for example, Marie Majerová, *Cesta blesku* (Path of the lightning) and *Sedm hrobů* (Seven graves); F. Halas, *Torso naděje* (Torso of hope); V. Nezval, *Historický obraz* (Historical image); S. K. Neumann and F. Jungmann, eds., *Československý podzim: Výbor z poezie 1938* (Czechoslovak autumn: a selection of poetry, 1938) (Prague, 1938); F. Valouch, *Česká poezie v období Mnichova* (Czech poetry of the Munich period) (Olomouc, 1970); Věra Holá and others, eds., *Mnichov: Vzpomínková kronika* (Munich: a chronicle of memoirs) (Prague, 1969); and Křen's evocative, somewhat Communist-slanted description of the "Munich Complex," *Do emigrace*, 85–109. See also F. Kubka, *Mnichov* (Munich) (5th ed., Prague, 1978), a widely read novel about a Czechoslovak journalist drifting about Europe's diplomatic capitals at the time.

6. See, for example, documentary collections such as: *Mnichov v dokumentech* (Munich in documents), 2 vols. (Prague, 1958); V.F. Klochko and others, eds., *New Documents on the History of Munich* (Prague, 1958); and criticisms of this collection by F. Vnuk in the *Journal of Central European Affairs* 21 (1961), and William V. Wallace in *International Affairs* 35 (1959); *Die Deutschen in der Tschechoslowakei, 1933–1947* (Prague, 1964); K. Gajan and R. Kvaček, eds., *Germany and Czechoslovakia, 1918–1948* (Prague, 1965); and Václav Král, ed., *Das Abkommen von München 1938: Diplomatische Dokumente aus den Jahren 1937–1939 aus tschechoslowakischen Archiven* (Prague, 1968). Věra Olivová's *The Doomed Democracy: Czechoslovakia in a Disrupted Europe, 1914–1938* (London, 1972) and Alice Teichová's *An Economic Background to Munich: International Business and Czechoslovakia, 1918–1938* (London, 1973) are surveys by "liberalized" communists. See also, *Lectures on the History of Munich* (Prague, 1959). There is no comprehensive bibliography of Czechoslovak publications on Munich in any language, although a "world bibliography" on the subject was to be prepared for the international conference on "Europe and Munich," held in Czechoslovakia in September 1973. Despite its title, Otto Kimminich, ed., *Das Münchener Abkommen in der tschechoslowakischen wissenschaftlichen Literatur seit dem zweiten Weltkrieg* (Munich, 1968), a product of the Sudeten German Archive in Munich, is merely a collection of six articles, one by Kimminich himself and five by Czechoslovak authors (translated into German and reprinted), dealing with the juridical aspects of the Munich agreement. A penetrating survey of Czechoslovak communist historiography on Munich from 1948 to 1968 is Míla Lvová's "Dvacet let o Mnichovu v naší ideologii a vědě" (Twenty years of Munich in our ideology and scholarship), *Revue dějin socialismu* 9, no. 3 (1969): 323–61.

7. On this specific issue, see Antonín Šnejdárek, "The Participation of the Sudeten–German Nazis in the Munich Tragedy," *Historica* 1 (1959): 241–65; and J.W. Bruegel, *Czechoslovakia Before Munich: The German Minority Problem and British Appeasement Policy* (New York, 1973), written by a Moravian German active in Czechoslovak politics until 1938.

8. Here, see such works as Václav Kopecký, *Třicet let ČSR* (Thirty years of Czechoslovakia) (Prague, 1948); R. Beckmann, *K diplomatickému pozadí Mnichova* (The diplomatic background of Munich) (Prague, 1954); and especially the tirade by Václav Král, Marxist hack, manufacturer of historical documents, powerful Soviet protégé, constant sentinel against "German revanchism," *O Masarykově a Benešově kontrarevoluční protisovětské politice* (On Masaryk's and Beneš's counterrevolutionary, anti-Soviet policy) (Prague, 1953), of which an impressive 31,000 copies were printed. Other early communist "exposés" are Zdenek Fierlinger, *Zrada československé buržoasie a jejich spojenců* (The betrayal of the Czechoslovak bourgeoisie and its allies) (Prague, 1951); Jan Křejčí, *Na nepřemožitelné frontě* (On the unconquerable front) (Prague, 1954); Jiří Pražák, *Nepřítel mezi hradbami* (Enemy within the walls) (Prague, 1956); Jan Křen, *Mnichovská zrada* (Munich betrayal) (Prague, 1958); and V. Král, *Politické strany a Mnichov* (Political parties and Munich) (Prague, 1961).

9. It is represented by such works as J.S. Hájek, *Mnichov 1938* (Munich 1938) (Prague, 1958); R. Kvaček, *Osudná mise* (Fateful mission) (Prague, 1958); and M. Lvová and J. Novotný, eds., *Chtěli jsme bojovat* (We wanted to fight) (Prague, 1963), 2 vols. documents.

10. R. Kvaček, *Nad Evropou zataženo* (Overcast Europe) (Prague, 1966), dealing with

European international affairs, 1933–37; Alena Gajanová, *ČSR a středoevropská politika velmocí, 1918–1938* (Czechoslovakia and the Great Powers' Central European policy) (Prague, 1967).

11. Translated by Svatopluk Pacejka (Editions Stock).

12. *From Munich to New War and New Victory*, trans. G. Lias, was published in Boston in 1965. The London version was edited by Beneš's wartime secretary, Jaromír Smutný, and disseminated by the Dr. Edvard Beneš Institute. It was described and analyzed in Otakar Odložilík, "Edvard Beneš on Munich Days," *Journal of Central European Affairs* 16, no. 4 (1957): 384–93.

13. Robert Littell, ed. (New York, 1960).

14. The same argument is made on the basis of a thorough examination of the relevant Czechoslovak archival materials by František Lukeš in "Poznámky k čs.–sovětským stykům v září 1938" (Notes on Czechoslovak–Soviet relations in September 1938), *Československý časopis historický* 16, no. 5 (1968): 703–31. Lukeš adds a plea to Soviet archivists and historians to supply more convincing materials, "if they exist."

15. Danica Kozlová, reviewing the film in *Tvorba*, 4 February 1973.

16. *Svět práce*, 18 April 1973.

17. "Historická literatura o Mnichovu 1938" (Historical literature on Munich 1938), *Československý časopis historický* 22, no. 1 (1974): 31–56. The same views are rendered in more popular form in Král's small paperback surveys of Munich, *Zářijové dny 1938* (September days of 1938) (Prague, 1971), and *Dny, které otřásly Československem* (Days that shook Czechoslovakia) (Prague, 1975).

18. See Otto Kimminich, "Das Münchener Abkommen in den deutsch-tschechoslowakischen Beziehungen seit 1945," *Donauraum* 17, no. 4 (1972): 185–200.

19. *Proč je Mnichov neplatný* (Why is Munich no longer valid) (Prague, 1971). For a summary and bibliography of world opinion on the legal nature of the Munich Pact, see Karin Schmid, "Synopsis der Meinungen zum Münchener Abkommen" (Cologne, 1972), 2 pts., *Berichte des Bundesinstituts für ostwissenschaftliche und internationale Studien* 7/1972.

20. D. Spáčil and V.F. Malcev, eds., *Dokumenty k historii Mnichovského diktátu, 1937–1939* (Documents on the history of the Munich dictate, 1937–1939) (Prague, 1979; and Moscow, 1979, in Russian).

21. Jarmila Wagnerová, ed., *Protifašistický boj a Mnichov* (Munich and the antifascist struggle) (Prague, 1979).

22. Robert Kvaček, *Historie jednoho roku* (The history of one year) (Prague, 1976); Karel Douděra, *Jak se rozhoupával zrady zvon* (How the bell of treason began to toll) (Prague, 1983).

23. See, for example, Václav Hyndrák, "K otázce vojenské připravenosti Československa v roce 1938" (The question of Czechoslovak military preparedness in 1938) in *Severní Čechy a Mnichov* (Munich and northern Bohemia) (Liberec, 1969), 140–75; Ladislav Deák, "Československo–sovietska spojenecka zmluva z r. 1935 a európska bezpečnost' " (The Czechoslovak–Soviet alliance treaty of 1935 and European security), *Slovanský Přehled* 59, no. 6 (1973): 456–64, 527–28; Václav Král, "Poznámky k úloze Sovětského Svazu v zářijové krizi v roce 1938" (Notes on the Soviet role during the September crisis), *Československo–sovětské vztahy* 1 (1972): 51–69; Jaroslav Mlýnský, "Československá–sovětská smlouva z r. 1935 a vztahy Československa k sovětské armádě" (The Czechoslovak–Soviet Treaty of 1935 and Czechoslovak relations with the Soviet army), *Časopis Matice Moravské* 94 (1975): 68–86; Robert Kvaček, "Vztahy mezi Československem a Sovětským svazem na jaře 1938" (Czechoslovak–Soviet relations in the spring of 1938), *Československo–sovětské vztahy* 3 (1974): 25–39; Václav Melichar, "Některé otázky obrany Československa v roce 1938" (Some issues concerning Czechoslovak defense in 1938), *Československý časopis historický* 22 no. 3 (1974): 321–28; Bohumil Plecitý, "Vztah Sovětského svazu k československé otázce v době ohrožení republiky hitlerovským Německem" (The relationship of the Soviet Union to the Czechoslovak question during the threat to the Republic by Hitler's Germany), *Protifašistický boj a Mnichov* (The antifascist fight and Munich) (Prague, 1979), 75–

108; and Miroslav Honzík et al., *Zněl zrady zvon* (The bell of treason tolled) (Prague, 1988). Particularly valuable are the detailed studies of the military preparedness and defensive capabilities of the Czechoslovak army by František Nesvadba, "Cesta čs. buržoazní armády k Mnichovu" (The path of the Czechoslovak bourgeois army to Munich), *Historie a vojenství* 32, no. 6 (1983): 70–91, and 33, no. 1 (1984): 66–86; "Čs. buržoazní armáda a obrana země proti agresi fašistického Německa v roce 1938" (The Czechoslovak bourgeois army and the defense of the country against the aggression of fascist Germany in 1938), *Historie a vojenství* 32, no. 1 (1983): 101–21, and no. 2: 3–20; and Nesvadba, *Proč nezahřměla děla* (Why the guns failed to thunder) (Prague, 1986).

24. Meanwhile, there is a small but interesting, informed, and perceptive volume of writing on the subject by Czechoslovak historians and intellectuals working outside Czechoslovakia, including Johann W. Bruegel, Ivan Pfaff, Eduard Táborský, Pavel Tigrid, and Jiří Hochman.

25. *O Smyslu českých dějin* (The meaning of Czech history) (Prague, 1953), 49.

4

The Diplomacy of Edvard Beneš: Munich and Its Aftermath

Michael Kraus

This chapter examines some of the main factors that shaped the perceptions and impinged upon the decision making of Edvard Beneš, the chief architect of Czechoslovak diplomacy in the 1930s and the country's leader from 1935 to 1938.[1] There is initially an overview of Czechoslovak–German relations; then, key facets of Beneš's diplomatic strategy are presented. An examination of Soviet diplomatic behavior as viewed from Prague follows, and, finally, there is a discussion of the impact of the Munich Pact on both Czechoslovakia and Beneš.

No element was as central to the stability and security of the new Czechoslovak state as the status of German–Czechoslovak relations. Consisting of two separate but interdependent spheres—internal and external—the uneasy relationship reflected the problems of an earlier era. Whereas the internal sphere was concerned with the presence of a substantial German minority (approximately 22 percent of the total population), the external concerned the relations with Germany—the neighboring great power that historically had dominated the Czech lands.

A key facet of German political psychology after 1918 was the reversal of status from that of the dominant nationality of the Austro-Hungarian Empire to a minority in a polity dominated by the once subordinate Czechs. (The same, though to a lesser extent, was true of the Hungarians vis-à-vis the Slovaks.) Small wonder that in 1918 most Sudeten German deputies opposed incorporation into the new Czechoslovak state. In the following years, mutual perceptions continued to reflect the cultural stereotypes of the Imperial era. In the words of a moderate Sudeten German, his people were prone to view the Czech as "a half-educated . . . creature, to some extent saved by German influence, who is politically intolerable and unreliable, socially never satisfied and always pushing for his nation." The Czech, our source informs us, saw "in the German the invader, the remorseless conqueror, the apostle of German world hegemony, who only lives in the land in order to subjugate the Czech people socially, politically, and in every other way."[2]

Because of geographical and demographic factors, the German question was at the heart of Czech national existence. To quote from a perceptive report by Walter Koch, the German minister in Prague, it posed the problem of survival for "an intelligent, hard-working, nationally very conscious people of 6–7 million, enclosed on three sides by about 70 million Germans."[3] Nor was the situation of the Sudeten Germans in interwar Czechoslovakia a typical case of an underprivileged, exploited minority, faced with discrimination and completely lacking in access to political institutions. As Koch himself pointed out in a dispatch to Berlin in the mid-1920s, an "ethnic group which numbers 3½ million in a population totaling 14 million, lives in compact ethnic areas, is culturally superior to the majority nation, produces the highest taxable incomes, and owns the greater part of industrial wealth, is really not a minority in need of protection, but an essential part of the state."[4] And if "it is united and can make its impact felt on the basis of the constitution," the German envoy concluded, "no one will be able to prevent it from obtaining its rights in the long run." As if to heed these words, German Social Democrats and other moderate German parties accepted the framework of the First Republic, and, by the mid-1920s, began to participate in the string of coalition governments in Prague.

Yet, contrary to Koch's expectations, German–Czech coexistence would have no "long run." What disrupted the relatively amicable course of German–Czechoslovak relations in the Weimar era was the combined impact of the depression and Nazism.[5] Growing unemployment—to cull the most visible aspect of the world economic crisis—had deleterious consequences for the fragile fabric of ethnic relations throughout the country. In Slovakia, for example, the discontent manifested itself in the rising stock of the People's Party, whose platform demanded Slovak autonomy from Prague (while its more radical wing favored complete independence). The heavily industrialized German districts were especially hard hit by the disruptive consequences of the depression in the early 1930s.[6] Nonetheless, it is doubtful that the economic hardships alone would have resulted in the radicalization of the Sudeten Germans. By the mid-1930s, the repercussions of the worldwide depression became inseparable from the impact of Hitler's seizure of power in Berlin.

After 1933, relations between Berlin and Prague deteriorated rapidly. In contrast to the Weimar governments, the Third Reich adopted an openly hostile policy toward Prague, encouraging irredentist demands among the Sudeten Germans and portraying Czechoslovakia, which had become a haven for refugees from Nazi Germany, as the bastion of Bolshevism in Europe. Beginning in 1934, the Nazis secretly financed the activities of the newly formed Sudeten German Homeland Front, headed by Konrad Henlein. Thus, the Sudeten German Party (SdP), as the Front was renamed, obtained the biggest campaign fund of all political parties on the Czechoslovak scene.[7] No less important to the rise of the SdP as a political force with a mass following was the nationalism in the neighboring "motherland." As a result, in the last prewar elections in 1935, Henlein's party received more than 60 percent of all German votes cast, which was approximately the same figure that the main government party, the Agrarians, received among the more numerous Czech voters. Significantly, in 1935, approximately one-third of the German votes still went to the parties supporting Czechoslovak democracy.[8] By the time local elections were held in May 1938, however, the SdP carried more than 78 percent of all German votes.[9] Inevitably, these results emboldened Henlein, and severely constrained Prague's ability to find a solution to the German question.

In the course of 1937–38 the Prague government held talks with Henlein's party in an attempt to contain the brewing crisis and accommodate legitimate German demands. Unknown to the Czechs, however, the search for a modus vivendi was doomed from the outset. In November 1937, Hitler had already informed his war and foreign ministers of his intention to conquer Czechoslovakia and Austria. Accordingly, directives went out to German armed forces to prepare for an "aggressive war against Czechoslovakia." Moreover, as Hitler pointed out during the November meeting, the crux of the Czechoslovak nationality problem was not the German minority, but the Czechs, who would have to be expelled.[10] This definition of the situation also affected Hitler's talks with his junior partner Henlein in March 1938 concerning the SdP's negotiations with Prague. The Hitler–Henlein talks produced the conspiratorial agreement "always [to] demand so much that we can never be satisfied."[11] In sum, from Hitler's point of view, the plight of the Germans in Czechoslovakia was merely a pretext for the primary goal of German conquest of Czechoslovakia. In 1938, however, as the leading diplomats in London and Paris entertained the demands of the Hitler–Henlein axis, they understood neither the tactics nor the objectives of the German dictator.

The crisis with Germany came as no surprise to Beneš. As Tomáš Masaryk's foreign minister of seventeen years, Beneš had exerted no small effort to stem the tide of German expansionism, which was the common denominator of his extensive diplomatic activities in the

League of Nations, as well as the motivating factor for the mutual defense treaties with France in 1924 and the Soviet Union in 1935. Earlier in 1935, the French had signed a treaty of alliance with Moscow, committing both parties to assistance in the event of unprovoked aggression. Prague followed in the footsteps of Paris, entering into a similar treaty with Moscow—one whose implementation was contingent upon the simultaneous action of France. Significantly, the linkage between the two pacts, which effectively weakened the Soviet obligation to assist Czechoslovakia, was added in compliance with Soviet wishes.[12] Moreover, the potential effectiveness of Soviet assistance was further circumscribed by geography because France and Czechoslovakia bordered on Germany, the presumed aggressor, whereas Russia did not. As later developments would demonstrate, neither Poland nor Romania (whose lands separated Czechoslovakia from the Soviet Union) was eager to permit Soviet troops to transit its territory.

By the time Beneš succeeded Masaryk as president in 1935, the Czechoslovak army had tremendously improved its resources and preparedness, and had become the best-trained and best-equipped military force in Central Europe.[13] Czechoslovakia's defense expenditures in 1936 constituted approximately 12.5 percent of its GNP—nearly the same as Germany's. Defense spending increased from 2,384 million crowns in 1935 to 5,274 million by 1937, when it amounted to almost 38 percent of the national budget.[14] The well-respected arms industry not only met many of the army's own needs, but also supplied an impressive weapons export program. The army's defense strategy depended upon an ambitious project of border fortifications and anticipated a retreat into Slovakia.

Despite the concerted efforts in defense, Czechoslovakia's armed forces were in a difficult predicament in September 1938. One need only review a few of the key constraints. First, the armament programs, including the construction of border defenses, were scheduled for completion only in 1942. Second, by adding 250 miles to the nearly 700-mile-long Czech border with Germany, the Anschluss of Austria in March 1938 dramatized the vulnerability of the Czechoslovak position, because no fortifications had been built along the Austrian border. To make matters worse, ideological and territorial disputes with Budapest and Warsaw turned borders with Hungary and Poland into security dilemmas as well. Moreover, Czechoslovakia's problem of defense was compounded by the multiethnic character of the state; the Czechs and Slovaks constituted a little less than 70 percent of the population. In the event of full mobilization, every fifth soldier and every tenth officer would be a German. Therefore, a conflict with the German or Hungarian neighbors probably would present a severe test of loyalty for some of the 250,000 German and Hungarian troops and 6,000 officers.[15]

Prague's diplomacy in the 1930s assumed that Czechoslovakia's independence was essential to maintaining the Versailles system, and that French and British concern about containing Germany gave those powers a vested interest in preserving the status quo in Central Europe. Accordingly, during the months leading to the Munich crisis, Beneš sought to persuade British and French diplomats that the concessions demanded by Hitler would paralyze Czechoslovakia and upset the balance of power in Central Europe, and, therefore, throughout Europe. Obviously, this was not a misguided tactic, especially when one considers that Czechoslovakia was much stronger militarily than Austria, and that its takeover would cause far greater harm to France and to European defenses against Germany.[16]

What the Czech leader failed to grasp, however, was that by September the British and French had subordinated their interest in maintaining the Versailles order to the overriding objective of avoiding war. After the Anschluss, Neville Chamberlain concluded that Czechoslovakia was militarily indefensible.[17] The ensuing divergence of purpose, it has been suggested, resulted in the contrasting definitions of the situation in the summer of 1938—the Czechs, led by Beneš, viewed the concessions to Germany in terms of preserving their relationship with the British and the French; the Western powers considered these concessions as a means of appeasing Germany.[18] As a result, two major concessions were made (to be sure, under great pressure) by the Czechoslovaks at an early stage of the crisis without sufficient attention to their full significance. The first was the acceptance of the Western powers as the interlocutors in the conflict with Germany, and the second concerned the willingness to cede territory. These concessions not only became the key ingredient of the Munich agreement, but, during the negotiations, they also formed a trap. In the words of David Vital:

> There was now no difference, except in tempo, between what the
> Germans demanded and what the British and the French
> required. The alliance with the West had been turned inside out
> and upside down. Instead of easing the German pressure on
> Czechoslovakia, the British and the French were adding to it.
> And because of the historical, ideological, and doctrinal aura the
> alliance bore in Czech eyes, the Western pressure was, if any-
> thing, more painful and more effective than the German.[19]

The pressure was more painful and more effective, one might add, because it was exerted by the powers that Prague had been accustomed to viewing as allies.

Yet, the alternative course of action—resisting the pressure from London and Paris—risked both loss of British and French support altogether and Czechoslovakia's complete isolation. It is, therefore, not surprising that, in the days preceding the Munich Conference, Beneš defined the "entire political problem" in terms of whether Hitler would be able to "isolate us, or whether we isolate Germany."[20] Still, Prague initially rejected the Anglo–French plan of 19 September, which was based on the Berchtesgaden terms, that called for ceding to Germany the districts with more than 50 percent German population. Only when Paris threatened Prague with the "responsibility for the provocation of German use of force" (and, therefore, with the abrogation of the French treaty obligations on assistance), did the Czechs reluctantly reverse their original decision.[21] Hitler's rejection of the Anglo–French plan at Godesberg on 23 September transformed the situation, however. Czechoslovakia declared a general mobilization, and the British and the French signaled that they would come to Prague's aid in the event of war, which was now considered a virtual certainty in all three capitals. But, in the last days of September, Chamberlain's quest for "peace in our time" led to the Munich Conference and, with it, the final humiliation of Prague.

What part did the Soviet Union assume in the events of the summer of 1938? A short answer is that Moscow played a secondary, if ambiguous, role. Russia was, of course, absolved of any formal obligation to Prague in the face of the French desertion. Nonetheless, the Kremlin maneuvered adroitly throughout the crisis, giving verbal support at various stages, and hinting (without any definite commitment) at the possibility of aiding Czechoslovakia even in circumstances in which France would not. So subtle and effective was Stalin's handling of the crisis that the question of Soviet diplomacy during the Munich crisis continues to be hotly debated.

In general, three interpretations have been advanced on the subject of Soviet assistance to Czechoslovakia. First, Moscow's official claim (supported by Soviet and orthodox Czechoslovak historians) has been that the Soviet Union was willing to provide aid to Czechoslovakia in September 1938, had Beneš requested it, despite the failure of France to do so.[22] The evidence for this claim has been so tenuous, however, that a Czech historian has demanded from Soviet scholars a disclosure of sources upon which they base this assertion.[23] According to the second view, Moscow was prepared to fulfill its obligations within the terms of the treaty, but the behavior of the Western powers preempted any effective aid.[24] Finally, the third position argues that no real assistance to Czechoslovakia was contemplated in September 1938. Recent research has unearthed no new evidence for the first claim and much support for the third. Thus, Jiří Hochman concludes his study on the note that the Soviet Union "was not willing and ready to help Czechoslovakia in any meaningful sense not only if France should abstain, but also if she should have upheld her treaty obligations."[25] Similarly, Ivan Pfaff has concluded that the Soviet Union "not only could not offer assistance, but above all, did not want to."[26]

Nonetheless, Stalin's diplomacy in September 1938 led Beneš and his compatriots to view the Soviet stance as the only bright spot in the entire international situation. Verbally, at least, the Russians appeared willing to honor their commitments. Moreover, when in September the Polish government threatened to resolve its long-running dispute with Prague over the Cieszyn (Teschen) district by force, Moscow warned Warsaw of the dire consequences of such an action and persuaded the Poles to restrain themselves, at least temporarily. For these reasons, Beneš publicly praised the Soviet stance of September 1938, and appeared confident that Moscow would fulfill the spirit of its treaty obligations. "We were certain," writes Beneš, "that they would fulfill their obligations and promises."[27]

The primary motivation on the part of Beneš for making such statements while in office was to maintain good relations with Moscow. By contrast, among trusted confidants, he admitted to the end his uncertainty about the form and the extent of Soviet military aid. Despite several enquiries about this question, the Czech leader received no firm commitment from the Russians on Soviet assistance in the event of France's failure to go to war.[28] In fact, as has been learned quite recently, he complained privately about Soviet diplomatic machinations. On the crucial night of 19 September after he received the so-called Anglo–French plan, Beneš requested that Soviet Ambassador Sergei Alexandrovskii urgently explore his government's position on the issue of Soviet assistance. After Alexandrovskii implored the Czechoslovaks to stand up firmly to Berlin, Beneš confided to Prokop Drtina, a close aide, his view of the Russians: "They, too, play a game of their own. We cannot trust them without reservations." And, considering the possibility of war, he added: "If they should get us into it, they will leave us in it."[29]

For all these reasons, Beneš decided not to risk a war against Germany with Russia as his only potential ally. Evidently, he feared the prospect of a war with Germany in which Czechoslovakia received only limited Soviet aid on the model of the Spanish Civil War.[30] Moreover, as some

members of the Prague cabinet stated openly, Czechoslovak armed resistance backed only by Russia would be viewed by the rest of Europe
as a "war of Bolshevism against Europe," which would bring "us into
open enmity with the Western world."[31] Alexandrovskii, who saw the
Czech leader often during the September crisis, characterized Beneš's
ambivalence toward Russia in a dispatch to Moscow on 29 September
1938:

> As far as Soviet assistance is concerned, Beneš would want it, on
> the one hand, but he is also afraid of it, on the other. . . . In our
> most recent talks, he always desperately grasped at the possibili-
> ties of our assistance and he called me in especially whenever he
> received another blow from England or France. But as soon as he
> recovered somewhat, or when he thought that he found another
> solution to the situation by means of a new diplomatic move, he
> would show much less interest in our stance.

The ambassador went on to portray Beneš in unflattering terms:

> I do not doubt for a moment that this dry pedant and clever dip-
> lomat from the very beginning to the end relied and still relies on
> the prospect of getting the most for Czechoslovakia by leaning on
> England and France, while he considers Soviet assistance as a
> means of defending Czechoslovakia against Hitler's offensive as
> quite suicidal for the Czechoslovak bourgeoisie.[32]

But Alexandrovskii, who appealed to his government after Munich "to
act more energetically" on Czechoslovakia's behalf, even at the cost of
confrontation with Hitler, was a poor judge of Stalin's intentions.[33] As
conspicuous a source as *Pravda* from 21 September 1938 offered important clues to the thinking in the Kremlin: "The Soviet Union takes
a calm view of the question of which imperialist predator rules in this
or that colony, this or that dependency, for it sees no difference between
German or British predators." And the very next day, *Pravda* declared
that the world was on the verge of "a second imperialist war." For the
initiated, *Pravda*'s definition of the impending war as "imperialist" signaled war in which the Soviet Union would not participate. Moreover,
although Moscow encouraged Prague to request Soviet assistance via
the cumbersome mechanism of the League of Nations, the declining
esteem in which Moscow held the League was evident in September, on
the occasion of the publication of the *Short Course*, the work whose preparation Stalin closely supervised. Its virtual omission of the policy of
collective security and its dim view of mutual assistance pacts spoke
loudly and clearly.[34]

In light of the foregoing evidence, it would appear that Moscow's main objective in September 1938 was to stay out of the impending war. (Certainly, the same was true of London and Paris.) Stalin's diplomacy during Munich, however, specifically Soviet encouragements to Beneš to stand firm against German demands in the absence of any clear Soviet military commitments, also suggests that Moscow attempted to deflect the war from Russia's borders by getting the Czechs "into it" early. It seemed quite plausible in the ensuing circumstances that a Czechoslovak–German war, by changing public opinion (and possibly governments) in London and Paris, would embroil Hitler in a war with the West, which would provide the Soviet Union with the much needed breathing space.[35]

There were two reasons that Beneš was the key decision maker on the Czechoslovak scene during the crisis. The first had to do with his undisputed authority in foreign affairs—Czechoslovakia's foreign policy had been his prerogative since 1918, and Beneš did not relinquish the control over policy making in this area even after he assumed the presidency. The other related reason stemmed from the fact that the government (cabinet) deferred to the president's judgment throughout the critical weeks of that summer. Although consultations between the castle, the cabinet members, the leaders of the coalition parties, and the military were held continuously, the available evidence suggests that Beneš's views prevailed at every stage of the confrontation, even when they were unpopular.

The key role Beneš played in the decision making during the crisis was also recognized in London and Paris. During September, communications from both governments were addressed to Beneš rather than to the cabinet. Furthermore, in the ensuing crisis, the voices advocating resistance grew louder than the argument—advanced mainly by Beneš—counseling submission. Therefore, Czechoslovakia accepted the Munich dictate primarily because Beneš prevailed upon the cabinet and the military to do so.[36] This conclusion, however, tells us nothing about the constraints under which the decision was made.

As the crisis between Czechoslovakia and Germany rushed toward its final denouement at Munich, Prague found itself not only diplomatically isolated, but also threatened by hostile neighbors. Warsaw and Budapest, pressing their territorial claims, left Prague in the unenviable position of having virtually no secure borders—in addition to the 950 miles of the Czech–German frontier, there were another 800 miles with Poland and Hungary to worry about. In the end, the choice was stark and clear to all—fight or surrender. Czechoslovak public opinion strongly favored armed resistance. "The great majority of the nation preferred war to capitulation," affirms one well-informed participant.[37] And the same held true for the leadership of the army.

While the conference in Bavaria was still in session, Beneš received a delegation of his ranking military commanders, including the prime minister (who was, since Berchtesgaden, also a general) and the chief of the general staff. Previously, their estimates had informed the president that the country could be defended against Germany for four to six weeks. But now they came to argue the case for resistance at any price. According to Beneš's own (posthumously published) account of the meeting, the generals implored him: "We must go to war, whatever the consequences. If we do, the big Western powers will be compelled to follow. The nation is absolutely united; the army is firm and wants to march. And even if we remain alone, we must not let go, the army has the obligation to defend the republic's territory, it wants to and will fight."[38] In reply, Beneš stated that he had to consider more than just "the sentiments of the nation and the army. I must take into account our entire internal and international situation, all aspects of what is involved, and all consequences stemming from our possible actions." He saw no grounds for the generals' optimism concerning Britain and France. On the contrary, he explained, "both of these countries will not go to war on account of Czech Germans, and if we do alone, they will hold us responsible for the war." Yet "war, a great Europe-wide war, is coming along with great upheavals and revolutions," he argued. In such circumstances it "would be irresponsible to lead the nation to a slaughterhouse now in an isolated war." Speaking of the Western allies, he stated: "If they don't want to fight with us, and under advantageous conditions, they will have to fight harder, and for us, when we no longer can."[39]

A call to resistance also came from the newly formed Committee for the Defense of the Republic, which was a group of politicians spanning a wide spectrum of views from left to right. Among the committee's most resolute advocates of resistance were the communists. During the municipal elections held in May, communist candidates fared well in most industrial and urban centers, especially in Prague where they became the second strongest party. Although they acted in concert with Soviet interests, their march behind the banner of patriotism clearly left its mark. In September communist leader Klement Gottwald made an eloquent case for self-defense on behalf of his party: "Barefoot Ethiopians, without arms, defended themselves, and we yield," he told Beneš, imploring him to reverse the decision to capitulate. Another member of the committee reminded Beneš that Masaryk "taught [the nation] that death was better than slavery. People cannot understand why we give away part of our territory without fighting." To these arguments, Beneš had only one answer: "We are alone and encircled on all sides. It would mean the death of the nation, and the nation must live!"[40]

There are those who have equated Beneš's stand with a failure of nerve and a lack of resolve. His capitulation to the decisions made at Munich, notes an account representative of this school of thought, was a "profound failure of psychological and political nerves."[41] Albeit superficially persuasive, this explanation does not withstand closer scrutiny. After all, on Beneš's orders, Czechoslovakia mobilized its army twice during the crisis and prepared for war. But the war Beneš contemplated was, in his mind, always linked to the actions of France, Czechoslovakia's closest ally. Conversely, for reasons already outlined, he was unprepared to wage a war without France, especially when Moscow showed a most reserved attitude. Moreover, the "failure of psychological and political nerves" explanation squares poorly with Beneš's actual behavior in September. Instead of hiding behind the constitutional cloak of limited presidential powers as he might have done, he took charge of the decision-making apparatus in the crisis and did not vacillate in his decision once he made it. Furthermore, as one of the republic's "founding fathers," Beneš could not take lightly the idea of capitulation to Berlin. It signified—or so it seemed—an ignominious end to the young state that he and Masaryk labored so hard to build. It also appeared to bring Beneš's brilliant political career to an abortive end. Having made the decision to capitulate, Beneš prepared immediately to abdicate the presidency. Arguably, in the given circumstances, the decision to capitulate to Hitler's demands was the more difficult road to take, especially as the voices of resistance grew louder—at least that is the view of some of Beneš's collaborators. According to Drtina, who disagreed with the decision to capitulate,

> For Dr. Beneš, it would have been much easier to go along with the demands of the Czech public than to resist and refuse them. That he did not avail himself of this simpler and for him an easier and more favorable possibility showed how seriously, responsibly . . . he evaluated the whole situation and the degree of personal courage that backs his stand and conviction. After all, it was clear that by going against the stream he risked his prestige, popularity and even the presidential office itself.[42]

Critical to an understanding of Beneš's reasons for the capitulation is the link he made between Paris and Prague as well as his conviction that the outbreak of an all-European war was inevitable. Simply put, as France went, Czechoslovakia would follow. Along the same lines, Beneš considered the acceptance of the Munich agreement as a temporary retreat in the face of an approaching war. In September 1938, under great pressure, Beneš traded space for time—Czechoslovakia would cede to Germany the border districts Hitler demanded in exchange for the security guarantees provided by Britain and France to protect the integrity of the rest of Czechoslovakia's territory. On the assumption that war would break out shortly, Czechoslovakia would enter it in a better physical state than otherwise, with its army intact. Weighing the perceived costs of the alternative—lone resistance—Beneš concluded that it was better to refrain from taking the nation into an unequal battle today when tomorrow's war should bring yesterday's allies to their senses.

As a result of the Munich Conference, Czechoslovakia lost 34 percent of its population (including more than one million Czechs and Slovaks), 29 percent of its territory, and 40 percent of its industrial capacity.[43] In addition to suffering large industrial losses, it forfeited the formidable fortifications in the border areas. Hitler's victory also opened the floodgates on the muddy waters of discontent from other channels. Poland and Hungary now seized the opportunity and grabbed the Czechoslovak territories they had previously coveted—the former appropriated the Teschen districts, and the latter seized southern Slovakia. Moreover, encouraged by the Germans, Slovak and Ruthenian nationalists demanded—and received—provincial autonomy from Prague. At the same time, Berlin called for the ouster of Jews from Czechoslovak government offices, and proceeded to dictate Prague's foreign policy. In October the Communist Party was banned, and the Social Democratic Party dissolved itself. Strict censorship was imposed on the press. Finally, to complete the humiliation, Hitler forced Beneš—who had resigned on 5 October—to leave the country at the end of the month.[44] Thus, Central Europe's only "bastion of democracy," as Czechoslovakia's First Republic has been called, collapsed like a house of cards. The collapse came—not because of its own defective weight, although defects existed—but principally owing to the impact of the external blows that where inflicted by enemies and allies alike.

This is not, however, the way in which matters were viewed by the recriminative postmortems in post-Munich Czechoslovakia. Whether measured by the unexpected behavior of Czechoslovakia's democratic allies or by the violation of traditional values and political symbols that Czechoslovakia had associated with their own political system and leadership, the events stretching from the Munich Conference to the imposition of the protectorate in March 1939 were a shattering experience for this twenty-year-old democracy. The spontaneous removal of pictures of Masaryk and Beneš from public offices provided only the most dramatic example of public sentiment. Prague, reported a Western journalist on the scene, became "a city hushed in grief."[45]

More salient were the observations drawn by George Kennan, the young American diplomat who arrived in Prague on the day of the Munich Conference. Can anyone "conceive of the chaos which the Munich catastrophe created in political life and political thought in Czechoslovakia?" he wondered. "Every feature of liberalism and democracy, in particular, was hopelessly and irretrievably discredited," Kennan observed in December 1938.[46] In Bohemia, a "silent but intense battle is taking place in every corner of the country and in every section of society between the old ideology and the new. If this is the death struggle of democracy in Bohemia, as many fear," he noted a short time later, "it can at least be said that democracy is dying hard." Indeed, as another observer put it, "Democratic Czechoslovakia was, in the last resort, a victim of democracy."[47] In sum, the post-Munich period in Czechoslovakia witnessed an agonizing crisis of legitimacy of the entire edifice of the First Republic, a reassessment of the institutions and practices of democracy, and a reappraisal of the country's international position, including alliances.

When Beneš made his decision, he correctly anticipated the imminent outbreak of war. Looking back, however, the Czech leader appears to have miscalculated in two ways. Hitler occupied the rest of the Czech lands in March 1939 and established the protectorate of Bohemia and Moravia as part of the Greater German Reich, which thereby extinguished what was known as the Second Republic. In doing so, he undermined much of Beneš's original rationale for accepting the Munich dictate—the preservation of the nation and the army for a more opportune battle. Simultaneously, Hungary, still trying to digest what it had taken in October, seized Ruthenia, while Hitler gave an ultimatum to the leading Slovak chauvinists to create their own "independent" state under German protection, or else. Beneš could hardly take comfort in the fact that one of the best-equipped armies in Europe fell without firing a shot. The formidable munitions factories in Czechoslovakia now furnished supplies to Hitler's war machine. Second, and no less important, in September 1938 the Czech leader failed to heed the warning from various political circles that the capitulation to German aggression would have a profoundly demoralizing impact on the national psychology.

While the British and French were busy congratulating each other on averting war, as far as the Czechs were concerned, the war with Germany had already begun. After March 1939, the Czechs were possibly the only people in Europe anxious for the war to spread. At that time, no one suspected that, once it engulfed the world, the war would not quickly end German domination—nor did anyone realize that peace would come to Prague later than anywhere else in Europe.

Considering that he was Munich's most immediate victim, it is hardly surprising that Beneš was traumatized by the experience. Rarely has a politician witnessed so complete a collapse of his policies as Beneš was forced to confront in the aftermath of September 1938. Moreover, Hitler's March 1939 occupation would inevitably reopen the question of capitulation. By his own admission, "this was a terrible blow to me: the entire structure of my future plans disintegrated . . . appeared finished."[48] Beneš, in fact, would spend the war years pondering the Munich disaster—reevaluating his own actions; reexamining every step he had taken. What some have called Beneš's "Munich complex," however, transcended personal tragedy.

Political crises can have a formative influence in shaping a political culture by strengthening or weakening certain elements in that political culture. The influence of such crises may prove more or less enduring. In the retrospective assessments of Czech historians, Munich, even more than the war itself, has come to be viewed as a turning point. In the words of one historian who has grappled with Beneš, Munich represents a "giant explosion . . . politically, in the realm of ideas, and morally, of our whole society."[49]

As a student of sociology and history, Beneš was not unaware of the potential long-term impact of his actions on his country's political culture. In fact, in the 1929 preface to *World War and Our Revolution,* Beneš had noted that national cultures are created gradually over a period of many generations and in relation to other cultures. Revolution and tradition have blended together in our recent past, he submitted, and the struggle for national liberation would assume an important place in the tradition of the new state. This theme led Beneš to make a more general observation concerning "collisions and struggles" with other nations that pose an existential challenge to the whole of a nation's being. "Such occasions," wrote Beneš, "become outstanding moments in the history of national life from which main elements of national traditions are created."[50] It is unclear whether or not he was conscious in September 1938 of the possibility that Munich would become such an "outstanding moment." What is certain is that after Munich the verdict of history about his own decision was never far from his mind.

"Ever since September, 1938, I kept thinking of it, literally day in and day out, I lived by it and suffered from it, and all of my political actions were directed toward" the undoing of Munich, recalled Beneš in his memoirs. "Indeed, it was the only purpose of my life."[51] Those who worked with Beneš during the war have also noted his constant preoccupation with Munich.[52] Referring to Beneš's "Munich complex," Edvard Táborský, his wartime personal secretary, suggests that Munich "affected his subsequent actions and policies." But, noting that Beneš later "began to view his actions as a great achievement of which he could be proud," Táborský concludes that it "influenced his views on Czechoslovakia's East-West relations considerably less than is generally believed."[53]

There is no doubt that Beneš wanted—and eventually claimed—to feel "proud of Munich." In fact, by 1944, he went as far as to say: "I consider that my behavior over Munich was the greatest achievement of my life."[54] Unlike Táborský, one need not simply accept at face value Beneš's own words on this score, not only because they were addressed to his authorized biographer, but also because other evidence from Beneš contradicts the picture of proud accomplishment. Although he always defended his decision in public, we know that privately he was haunted by gnawing doubts: *"Did I decide in that terrible crisis correctly? Will not the events that ensued condemn me?"* he asked on one of the last pages of his memoir, which he could not bring himself to publish in his lifetime.[55] Moreover, on psychological, no less than on political, grounds it is difficult to conceive of any statesman who, having capitulated to foreign aggression, would take pride in his decision to do so, whatever the circumstances. Furthermore, Beneš could never escape the voices of skeptics around him, who, by questioning the Munich decision, would reignite his own doubts. Because such critics, in addition to assorted Czechoslovak elements, also included Churchill and Stalin, Beneš could take little comfort in his September 1938 judgment. Thus, Jaromír Smutný's observation made in August 1943 seems much closer to the mark than Táborský's conclusion: "For the president . . . ," noted the head of his office, "there is no escape from the knowledge that Munich was a *personal* defeat for him, a *personal* humiliation, and a defeat of his own personal policy."[56]

Of particular significance for our purposes, however, is the question of how the "Munich complex" influenced the pattern of Beneš's wartime diplomacy and the course of postwar developments. In a 1944 conversation with his authorized biographer, Beneš provided a key clue to his wartime efforts: "From September 30, 1938, I never stopped thinking, day and night, how to achieve the repudiation of that despicable Munich dictate. . . . I lived with one single aim in my life—the repudiation of Munich and the reconstitution of the Czechoslovak republic."[57] After Munich, Beneš's direction at the helm of the wartime government in exile gradually came to envision a new Central Europe, in which Moscow would play the role of interwar France as a counterweight to Germany and a guarantor of stability and independence.

This attitude—underpinned by Beneš's belief in East-West convergence—helps to explain the reason that he welcomed common borders with Russia, and it sheds light on Beneš's negotiations in Moscow in December 1943 and March 1945. During these visits, he more or less volunteered to subordinate Prague's foreign policy to Soviet interests, pledged that the communists would be included in every future government, and accepted virtually every point in their postwar program. In return, Beneš received Moscow's support for what by 1943 had become the linchpin of his postwar plans, the expulsion of the Sudeten Germans. In short, to achieve his goal of "undoing" Munich, he initiated a courtship with another disaster.[58]

NOTES

1. Portions of this paper draw on my Ph.D. dissertation, *The Soviet Union, Czechoslovakia and the Second World War: The Foundations of Communist Rule*, Princeton University, 1986. I am indebted to Katerina Kraus of Princeton University's Firestone Library for research assistance and to the Institute for Sino-Soviet Studies, George Washington University, which sheltered me while I prepared the final version of this manuscript.
2. Quoted in Elizabeth Wiskemann, *Czechs and Germans* (London, 1938), 118.
3. J. W. Bruegel, *Czechoslovakia before Munich* (Cambridge, 1973), 71.
4. Ibid., 73.
5. The best-documented study of German–Czechoslovak relations in the pre-Hitler era is F. Gregory Campbell, *Confrontation in Central Europe: Weimar Germany and Czechoslovakia* (Chicago, 1975).
6. William Wallace, *Czechoslovakia* (Boulder, 1976), 192–93.
7. Bruegel, *Czechoslovakia before Munich*, 120, 213.
8. Ibid., 124.
9. Josef Korbel, *Twentieth Century Czechoslovakia* (New York, 1977), 119.
10. For more detail, see Gerhard L. Weinberg, *The Foreign Policy of Hitler's Germany: Starting World War II, 1937–1939* (Chicago, 1980), 34–42.
11. Bruegel, *Czechoslovakia before Munich*, 173.
12. See Jiří Hochman, *The Soviet Union and the Failure of Collective Security* (London and Ithaca, 1984), 53; Hochman disagrees on this point with Jonathan Haslam, who asserts that this "was a condition the Czechs were keen to see." See also Haslam, *The Soviet Union and the Struggle for Collective Security in Europe, 1933–1939* (New York, 1984), 51.
13. For two well-informed analyses of Prague's prospects to wage a defensive war against Germany, see Milan Hauner, "Září 1938: kapitulovat ci bojovat?" (September 1938: To capitulate or to fight?) *Svedectví* 49 (1975): 151–63; and Václav Kural, "Vojensky moment česko–německeho vztahů v roce 1938" (The military aspect of the Czech–German relationship in 1938), *Historické studie* 22 (Prague, samizdat, 1988): 66–112; for Beneš's activities as commander in chief, see Prokop Drtina, *Československo, můj osud* (Toronto, 1982), vol. 1, pt. 1, 65–70.
14. *Září 1938*, 156; Jan Anger, *Mnichov 1938* (Munich 1938) (Prague, 1988), 56.
15. These figures come from Hauner, *Září 1938*, 157, 171; Hauner's balanced reading of the evidence leads him to a generally skeptical view of Prague's military capabilities.

16. Telford Taylor, *Munich: The Price of Peace* (New York, 1980), 381.
17. Ibid., 628.
18. This argument is persuasively developed by David Vital, "Czechoslovakia and the Powers, September 1938," in *European Diplomacy Between Two Wars, 1919–1939*, ed. Hans Gattzke (Chicago, 1972), 195–96.
19. Ibid., 197.
20. Drtina, *Československo, můj osud*, 171.
21. Copy of the French memorandum is in Edvard Beneš, *Mnichovské dny* (Prague, 1968), 261–62.
22. For a recent example, see O. A. Rzhevskii, ed., *Pravda i lozh o vtoroi mirovoi voine* (Truth and lies about the Second World War) (Moscow, 1988), 36–38. The first occasion for this assertion was a 28 December 1949 *Pravda* article, according to which Gottwald delivered Stalin's message to Beneš in May 1938 to this effect. There are several sound reasons to question the veracity of this report. First, it would have been a most unusual departure for Stalin to use a communist leader as a channel of communication with another government, especially when the alleged offer had potentially far-reaching implications for Soviet policies; then, no such claims were made while Beneš—the only other witness—was still alive. Finally, the credibility of this story suffers from the fact that Ivan Maisky, the former Soviet ambassador to London, dates the transmission of the message to early September; see his *Who Helped Hitler?* (London, 1964), 79.
23. František Lukeš, "Poznámky k čs.-sovětským vztahům v září 1938," *Československý Časopis Historický* (May 1968): 703–31.
24. For a well-documented account adopting this perspective, see Haslam, *The Soviet Union and the Struggle of Collective Security*, esp. ch. 9.
25. Hochman, *The Soviet Union and the Failure of Collective Security*, 169.
26. See Ivan Pfaff, "Jak tomu opravdu bylo se sovětskou pomoci v mnichovské krizi" (What was really the nature of Soviet aid during the Munich crisis), *Svedectví* 56 (1978): 51–68; and 57 (1978): 566–85.
27. Beneš, *Mnichovské dny*, 324.
28. For a clear statement from Beneš on this score, see J.W. Bruegel, "Dr. Beneš on the Soviet 'Offer of Help' in 1938," *East Central Europe*, vol. 4, pt. 1, 1977; 56–59; also *Mnichovské dny*, 322.
29. Drtina, *Československo, můj osud*, 106; the author was Beneš's personal secretary before and during the war; in 1946–48, Drtina served as the Minister of Justice.
30. See Beneš's own observations in *Mnichovské dny*, 322.
31. Quoted in Pfaff, "Jak tomu opravdu bylo se sovětskou pomoci v mnichovské krizi," 62, n53.
32. *Dokumenty a materialy k dějinám československo–sovětských vztahů* (Documents and materials on the history of Czechoslovak–Soviet relations) (Prague, 1979), 3, 595–96.
33. He was recalled from Prague in 1939, arrested in 1943, and executed in 1945 allegedly for "high treason and espionage for fascist Germany." See *Rudé právo*, 9 August 1989.
34. For a well-informed assessment of Stalin's policies in the 1930s, see Robert C. Tucker, "The Emergence of Stalin's Foreign Policy," *Slavic Review* (December 1977), esp. 568–71, 587–89.
35. This, in any event, was Churchill's belief at the time; see his *The Gathering Storm* (Boston, 1948), 302.
36. This interpretation is supported by most testimonies, including Beneš's own; see his posthumously published memoir, *Mnichovské dny*, Prague 1968, esp. pp. 249, 254–55, 272; see also the recent revelations by Beneš's secretary Prokop Drtina, *Československo můj osud*, esp. vol. I, pt. I, 196–244; "It is clear that the decision to capitulate was almost entirely Beneš's," writes Korbel, *Twentieth Century Czechoslovakia*, 144.
37. Drtina, *Československo, můj osud*, 202; also 165; for evidence on public opinion, see 101–244.
38. *Mnichovské dny*, 340–41.

39. Ibid., 341–42.
40. Quoted in Korbel, *Twentieth Century Czechoslovakia*, 140–41.
41. Joseph Rothschild, *East Central Europe Between the Two World Wars* (Seattle, 1974), 132.
42. Drtina, *Československo, můj osud*, 140–41.
43. Wallace, *Czechoslovakia*, 214; Theodore Prochazka, *The Second Republic: The Disintegration of Post-Munich Czechoslovakia* (Boulder, 1981), 53.
44. For details, see Prochazka, ibid., esp. chs. II and III.
45. G. E. Gedye in *New York Times*, 1 October 1938.
46. George Kennan, *From Prague After Munich* (Princeton, 1968), 7.
47. Taylor, *Munich*, 1003.
48. Beneš, *Paměti*, 97.
49. Míla Lvová, "Dvacet let o Mnichovu v naší ideologii a vědě" (Twenty years of Munich in our ideology and scholarship), *Revue dějin socialismu* 3 (1969): 1; see also the chapter by Joseph Zacek in this volume.
50. Edvard Beneš, *Svetová válka a nase revoluce* (The world struggle and our revolution) (Prague, 1929), xi–xii.
51. Beneš, *Paměti*, 294.
52. In addition to references cited below, see, for example, Drtina, *Československo, můj osud*, 230–31; Ladislav Feierabend, *Beneš mezi Washingtonem a Moskvou* (Washington, D.C., 1966), 128–29.
53. *President Edvard Beneš* (Palo Alto, 1981), 29, 70–71.
54. Quoted in ibid., 71.
55. Beneš, *Mnichovské dny*, 342; emphasis in the original.
56. Libuse Otáhalová and Milada Červinková, eds., *Dokumenty z historie československé politiky 1939–43* (Documents from the history of Czechoslovak politics 1939–43) (Prague, 1966), I, Document no. 298: 362; emphasis in the original.
57. Compton Mackenzie, *Dr. Beneš* (London, 1946), 322.
58. For additional evidence for this interpretation, see note 1.

5

The View from Warsaw

Anna M. Cienciala

Polish policy during the Czechoslovak crisis, particularly the annexation of disputed territory after Munich, was widely condemned at the time, and the vast majority of Poles regret or condemn it today. Historians, however, should still make an effort to understand it. This chapter presents the policy goals of the decision makers in Warsaw and the assumptions upon which these goals were based. It is the view of this author, already presented elsewhere, that Polish policy in 1938 was largely determined by actual, as opposed to proclaimed, French and British policy toward the Czechoslovak crisis.[1]

Some background on Polish views of Czechoslovakia and the evolution of Polish foreign policy to 1938 is necessary before discussing Polish policy toward that country in 1938. Although the recovery of western Teschen Silesia—Zaolzie to the Poles and Teschen to Western observers—was not the principal goal of Polish policy at that time, it was a very emotional issue for most Poles. Zaolzie was generally understood to include most of the region West of the Olza river, stretching as far as the Ostravica river. Except for the westernmost areas, most of this territory was preponderantly Polish-speaking.[2] Educated Poles knew that a provisional demarcation line that allocated most of Zaolzie to Poland had been agreed upon by Polish and Czechoslovak local councils in November 1918. Some also knew that Józef Piłsudski's proposal to establish a mixed Polish–Czechoslovak commission to settle the boundary had been ignored by Prague. Most Poles deeply resented the Czechoslovak appropriation of Zaolzie in January 1919 and then its absorption into Czechoslovakia, without a plebiscite, by the Conference of Ambassadors in late July 1920.[3] Finally, they resented the Czech assimilationist policy in the region. In sum, Polish public opinion believed that a great injustice had been perpetrated and that Zaolzie must eventually return to Poland. This view was also held by opposition parties and groups otherwise critical of the government's foreign policy. The lone exception was the Polish Communist Party which was, however, too small to exert any influence in Poland, despite its troublesome presence on Czechoslovak territory in Zaolzie.[4] Thus, all the major opposition leaders who spoke with Dr. Václav Fiala—sent by President Edvard Beneš to Poland in April 1938 to learn what the opposition had to offer—asserted that the precondition for improved Polish–Czechoslovak relations, and possibly an alliance, was the return of Zaolzie to Poland. They also demanded that Czechoslovakia abrogate its 1935 alliance with the Soviet Union.[5]

Zaolzie, however, was not the only source of Polish grievances against Czechoslovakia. There was also the memory of Czechoslovak neutrality in the Polish–Soviet war of 1920 and of Prague's approval of German revisionist claims against Poland in the 1920s and early 1930s.[6] These grievances were compounded by the fact that Czechoslovakia had given asylum to many Ukrainian political refugees from former East Galicia and, after 1930, to Polish political refugees as well.

Still, it is important to remember that in 1925–33, the Poles tried to establish closer relations with their southern neighbor. Despite some promising military consultations, however, it was clear that Prague did not want to shoulder Poland's problems with Germany and was unprepared to go beyond a treaty of friendship.[7] Instead, Prague followed the French lead in signing an alliance with Moscow in May 1935. This was deeply resented in Poland, and Polish policy makers henceforth tended to view Czechoslovakia as an agent of the Soviet Union and the Comintern, and the Czechoslovak foreign minister (later president), Edvard Beneš, as a "lackey" of France. The real basis for these distorted views was the fear that France would abandon or subordinate its Polish ally to the Soviet Union, which meant returning to the old Franco–Russian alliance of 1894.

It was tragic that mutual distrust led Poland and Czechoslovakia to view each other as a *"Saisonstaat"*—a temporary state that could not last because of the potential internal and external dangers to which it was exposed. Thus, until 1933–34, Czechoslovak policy makers believed that eventually Poland would be forced to fight Germany or the Soviet Union or both, and that the Western Powers would not go to war to support Poland. The Czechoslovak government, therefore, refused to consider an alliance with Poland in 1933—precisely when the Poles might have welcomed it.[8] Both Józef Piłsudski, who exerted a dominant influence on Polish policy after his return to power in May 1926, and his disciple Józef Beck, who became foreign minister in December 1932, came to view Austria and Czechoslovakia as states that could not survive without the support of the Western Powers. They believed that this

support was most unlikely, however, in view of French and British con-
ciliatory policy toward Germany since the Locarno treaties of October
1925. Nevertheless, the French ambassador in Warsaw, Jules Laroche,
believed that Piłsudski and Beck would change their attitudes if France
drew the sword.[9]

At Locarno, France had signed mutual assistance treaties with Poland
and Czechoslovakia. Despite recognition of the previous alliances, however, these new treaties made mutual assistance (in effect, France's assistance to its allies) dependent on the League of Nations. The latter
was the basis of British policy in Europe, and French statesmen were
reluctant to undertake any action without British support or approval.
In Polish eyes, the Locarno treaties undermined the bilateral Franco–
Polish alliance of 1921.[10] Józef Piłsudski concluded that Poland must
balance this weakening of the Franco–Polish alliance by improving relations with the Soviet Union and even more so with Germany—thereby
removing the revision of the Polish–German frontier from the agenda
of any Western negotiations with Berlin. He achieved this goal by signing the Polish–German declaration of nonaggression on 27 January
1934, which balanced the Polish–Soviet nonaggression pact of 1932.
This was the policy of "equilibrium," which mandated good Polish relations with both old enemies without entering into close relations with
either.[11]

Piłsudski had no illusions, however, that he had found lasting guarantees for Poland's security. On the contrary, in the spring of 1934,
shortly after the signing of the Polish–German declaration of nonaggression, he asked his senior officers and top foreign ministry officials
to study the question: Which of Poland's two powerful neighbors would
be the first to attack it? Although most of the officers chose Germany,
Piłsudski believed it would be Russia. He reasoned that Hitler needed
a few years to consolidate his power, but that Stalin was unpredictable;
and Poland could depend upon outside aid in a war with Germany, but
not with Russia. Piłsudski predicted that Poland probably could count
on at most four years of peace, until 1938; therefore, he urged that it
make the best use of this time to grow stronger.[12]

Although the Franco–Polish alliance remained a pillar of Polish foreign policy, it also presented some uncertainty insofar as France was
following Britain in seeking a general settlement with Germany in Europe. It was no secret that most Western leaders believed that such a
settlement could not be achieved without revising the Polish–German
frontier, which Poland, naturally, adamantly opposed.[13] In addition, despite repeated Polish efforts, French governments, and, therefore, the
French general staff, were reluctant to define the actual implementation

of the Franco–Polish military convention of February 1921. Indeed, France even tried to dilute it, which Piłsudski refused to do.[14] In fact, not until May 1939 did the French general staff actually define what France would do to help Poland in the event of war. Even then France had no intention of fulfilling its commitment to launch a general offensive against Germany if the latter attacked Poland.[15]

Recalling all of these factors, in addition to the well-known Franco–British policy toward Germany in 1938, it is hardly surprising that the primary motivation of Polish policy at that time was to obtain some additional security from the reduction of Czechoslovak territory, which was, from the outset, considered likely if the Western Powers failed to support Prague. The British government was willing to do everything to avert war, which was a fact well known to Polish policy makers, who correctly assumed that Paris would continue to follow London's lead. Indeed, French Foreign Minister Georges Bonnet bluntly told the Czechoslovak minister in Paris, Stefan Osušky, on 20 July 1938, that under no circumstances would France go to war over the Sudetenland. Presumably, this declaration stemmed from the information—transmitted that day by British Foreign Secretary Lord Halifax—that he had just sent President Beneš a note demanding that he accept "the good offices" of Lord Runciman as mediator in the dispute between the Sudeten German leaders and Prague.[16] Bonnet's declaration to Osušky, however, remained a well-guarded secret, so most observers assumed that, if the unthinkable happened—if Germany attacked Czechoslovakia—France would be forced to fulfill its obligation to its ally by declaring war on Germany. In that contingency, it was assumed that Britain would also become involved; in such a situation, Polish policy makers maintained that Poland could not be on Germany's side. If the crisis were to be resolved peacefully, however, they intended to strengthen Poland's security. Consequently, Polish policy makers decided to remain open to one of two possibilities that all European governments had to consider—depending upon the outcome of the Czechoslovak crisis—peace or war.

It is incorrect to call Polish policy "the policy of Colonel Józef Beck." In fact, although Beck formulated Polish foreign policy, this policy needed the approval of an informal inner cabinet consisting of five men: Foreign Minister Beck; President Ignacy Mościcki; Mościcki's constitutionally designated successor in case of war, Marshal Edward Śmigły-Rydz, the inspector general of the Polish armed forces and commander in chief in case of war; Premier (General) Dr. Felicjan Sławoj-Składkowski; and President Mościcki's protégé, Deputy Premier and Minister of Finance Eugeniusz Kwiatkowski.[17] The five men met at the president's residence—the Royal Castle in Warsaw. Although there are few references to these meetings, and no records appear to have survived (except a personal one to be cited later), they were apparently convened to discuss and approve major policy decisions. The first such meeting was held shortly after Piłsudski's death, which occurred on 12 May 1935.

Thus, four goals of Polish foreign policy emerged in 1938. First, it can be assumed that all of the members of the inner cabinet agreed with Beck that the Western Powers, as well as the Soviet Union, were most unlikely to go to war with Germany over Czechoslovakia. Presumably, they also agreed with him that, whether or not Czechoslovakia was forced to grant autonomy to the Sudeten Germans or cede the Sudetenland to Germany, Poland should demand the same for Zaolzie.

Second, they certainly agreed on Beck's proposal to establish a common frontier with Hungary. This common frontier, which would be established by the Hungarian acquisition of Subcarpathian Ruthenia and the attachment of an autonomous Slovakia to Hungary, would form the basis for a new bloc to be called the "Third Europe." This bloc, Beck's idea, would include Poland, Romania, and Hungary, and its task would be to prevent further German or new Soviet expansion in eastern Europe. Beck hoped for the support of the Western Powers, or at least of Italy, since Mussolini and Ciano showed a lively interest in the establishment of a Warsaw–Budapest–Bucharest–Rome axis to prevent German domination of the western Balkans and Hungary. For Polish policy makers, the Third Europe was, in turn, connected with the goal of avoiding a solution that would place all of Czechoslovakia, with or without the Sudetenland, under German domination, for this would involve German encirclement of Poland. Thus, the Polish government demanded the same rights for the small Polish population of Zaolzie as those granted to the Sudeten Germans. For the same reason, Warsaw supported Hungarian claims to Subcarpathian Ruthenia and the creation of an autonomous Slovakia linked to Hungary.[18]

Third, Poland wanted to "sell" Polish neutrality to Germany in the presumably unlikely event of a local war. In return, Germany would formally recognize the Free City of Danzig and Polish rights there, and extend the Polish–German declaration of nonaggression of 26 January 1934.

Fourth, Polish policy makers agreed that Poland could not accept Great Power decisions on matters of vital interest to itself, if they were made without Polish participation. They vividly recalled the Four Power Pact of 1934, which was designed to establish a directory of great powers—Britain, France, Germany, and Italy—to settle disputes stemming from the peace settlements. Poland adamantly opposed this plan because it refused to consider any revision of the Polish–German frontier.

Three of the four objectives (except the Third Europe) had been part of Polish foreign policy for years. Although Piłsudski had been unwilling to undertake any commitment south of the Carpathian mountains, the idea of a Third Europe had its roots in the early 1920s, when Polish statesmen dreamed of creating a bloc of states, reaching from the Baltic to the Aegean, led by Poland. It must be emphasized that the policy goals concerning Zaolzie, German recognition of Danzig, and a Third Europe were to be realized only if the Czechoslovak crisis were resolved by a diplomatic arrangement without war. If Germany attacked Czechoslovakia, however, and if France should go to its aid, presumably with British support, Polish policy makers agreed that Poland could not be on Germany's side in an all-European war. Thus, Poland had to keep its options open until the resolution of the Czechoslovak crisis.

Beck describes this policy in his memoirs. At two successive Warsaw Royal Castle conferences in 1938, he outlined his basic hypotheses as follows: The Czechs would not fight; the Western Powers were unprepared, both morally and materially, to help the Czechs; and the Soviet Union would limit itself to mere demonstrations. At the same time, Beck insists that he always qualified these hypotheses by categorically stating that Poland could not, and should not, be the first to engage in any action against Czechoslovakia; if it came to war, however, Poland would have to change its policy within twenty-four hours, for, in a real European war against Germany, it could not find itself even indirectly on Germany's side.[19]

Of course, Beck's statements provide only the basic assumptions about Polish policy in 1938. He does not give exact dates for these conferences, although it may be assumed that this policy was formulated in early spring at the latest. Finally, there is no corroborating evidence from the other conference participants, which is not surprising because the meetings were secret. This explains most historians' disbelief that Poland would really have aligned itself with the Western Powers against Germany in the event of an all-European war. Yet, other evidence exists to support Beck's statements.

Documents of both Polish and other origin reveal that, even before 1938, Poland demanded the same concessions for the Polish minority in Czechoslovakia as might be granted to any other minority. It may be assumed that this demand, formulated in February 1937, reflected Polish fears that the Sudeten Germans might be given some rights not awarded the Polish minority.[20] This Polish stance would develop into official policy in late March 1938.

The information that Beck had in hand before the Czechoslovak crisis began is also available. In early December 1937, Berlin informed the Polish foreign minister of Lord Halifax's statement to Hitler at Berchtesgaden in November that Britain would not oppose peaceful changes in central Europe, specifically in Austria, Czechoslovakia, and Danzig. Then, from his talks with Hitler, Göring, Goebbels, and Foreign Minister von Neurath in Berlin on 13–14 January 1938, Beck learned of their determination to eliminate Czechoslovakia.[21] Finally, Beck knew that the Czechoslovak government was unwilling to undertake bilateral talks with Poland. According to Kazimierz Wierzbiański, the Polish press attaché in Prague, Beck made an informal inquiry in early January 1938, saying that if Prague presented a concrete agenda and not just meaningless proposals for cultural cooperation or permanent friendship, Warsaw would not reject it. This informal suggestion was transmitted to the Czechoslovak foreign ministry, the prime minister, and the chairman of the largest political party—the Agrarian Party. French circles in Prague were also informed. Ten days later, the Czechoslovak answer was negative. The Polish press attaché learned that Moscow had advised Prague not to accept the offer.[22] Although no other source has been found to confirm the Polish press attaché's information, it seems probable that Beck did make such a move, presumably in the hope of beginning talks with Prague on the Zaolzie problem before Hitler proceeded with his plan of eliminating Czechoslovakia. On 24 March, however, Prime Minister Neville Chamberlain declared in the House of Commons that Britain would give no guarantee to Czechoslovakia because this would take the decision of peace or war out of British hands and, in any case, Britain could not be committed to an area not vital to its interests. Although Chamberlain warned that if war broke out, it would probably not be confined to those who had assumed obligations, it was clear that Britain had no desire to risk a war with Germany over Czechoslovakia.[23]

It is not surprising, therefore, that Polish demands for Zaolzie in February 1937 were transmuted into policy a year later. On 29 March 1938, four days after Chamberlain's statement, the Polish minister in Prague, Kazimierz Papée, told Foreign Minister Kamil Krofta that Poland would demand the same concessions for the Polish minority in Czechoslovakia that would be made to any other minority group—in other words, the Germans.[24] In late March 1938, therefore, the Polish government adjusted its policy toward Czechoslovakia according to what it knew of the British attitude, which had been expressed confidentially by Halifax to Hitler in November 1937 and publicly by Chamberlain in March 1938. Polish policy also was based upon what was known about the German stance, which became apparent in January 1938, and finally on the knowledge that Czechoslovakia did not want to undertake talks with Warsaw about the Polish minority.

Of a long list of both Polish and non-Polish documents that could be cited in support of Beck's brief statement on Polish policy in 1938, a few have been selected for inclusion here. One is an intriguing account of Beck's views as forwarded to Paris by the French ambassador in Warsaw, Léon Noël, on 26 April 1938. According to a report from one of the ambassador's Polish "collaborators" of the latter's conversation with a highly placed Polish personage, whose functions put him in touch with the *dirigeants* of Poland, Beck was very worried about Poland's position following the Anschluss. He sought to build a barrier with Hungary and Romania against further German expansion. Beck believed, however, that everything depended on the Western Powers and that the key piece of the system—and the only power capable of containing German ambitions in Europe—was France. France, however, worried him because of its internal situation and of what he considered its pro-Russian tendencies.

Beck was said to envisage three scenarios for Czechoslovakia. (1) It would succeed in maintaining its frontiers at the price of extensive concessions to the German minority. In that case, Poland would limit itself to demanding equal treatment for the Polish minority. Beck considered this the most favorable solution for Poland and all the other countries; it was also the most difficult, because it would require strong Western solidarity and Soviet *désintéréssement*. (2) It would retain its frontiers and its superficial independence, but would become a kind of "*Deutsches Gebiet*" (German zone), as a result of Sudeten German preponderance in the government, and, perhaps, a customs union with Germany. Beck thought that this solution was favored at the time by the German foreign ministry, the army, and moderate elements in the Nazi party. He considered it, however, the most dangerous solution for Poland, which would then be completely encircled by Germany and limited in its contact with the rest of the world to the narrow isthmus of Romania. (Poland and Romania had a defensive alliance against the Soviet Union, and Romania had close relations with France.) (3) It would disintegrate as a result of a plebiscite in the Sudetenland, if extremist elements won in Berlin, or if it failed to retain even superficial sovereignty. In this case, Beck believed that Poland's priority would be to gain a common frontier with Hungary.

The Polish individual who gave this account to Noël's collaborator was struck by the fact that Beck appeared to consider the third scenario as the most likely. Therefore, the author of the report believed that a key task of the Polish ambassador to Romania would be to secure a general agreement between Romania and Hungary to resolve their disputes.[25] The veracity of this report is at least partly confirmed by the instructions that Undersecretary of State Jan Szembek gave on 18 April to the newly appointed Polish ambassador to Romania, Roger Raczyński. Szembek told him that he did not believe that the Western Powers would defend Czechoslovakia, and urged the ambassador to work for a Romanian–Hungarian understanding. Such an understanding would be vitally important in consolidating Polish influence in the region between Russia and Germany considering the new power system that would probably emerge. Szembek also expressed the belief that French influence would have to be neutralized and Czechoslovakia "routed." When Raczyński remarked, however, that complete Czechoslovak submission to German influence could not be prevented and that Germany would then proceed to destroy the Czechoslovak state, Szembek replied that this was not the Polish goal. On the contrary, he said that although this possibility was not out of the question, Polish policy would aim to use all available means to forestall such an eventuality.[26] Presumably, Szembek meant that Germany must be prevented from controlling or annexing the entire Czechoslovak state.

A second document illustrating Polish views on policy options in 1938 is a long report dated 19 June 1938, written by the U.S. ambassador in Warsaw, Anthony J. Drexel Biddle. It is noteworthy that Drexel Biddle enjoyed very good relations with Beck, who treated him both as a friend and a conduit for passing on his views and ideas to the American ambassador in Paris, William C. Bullitt. The latter, in turn, was close not only to President Franklin D. Roosevelt but also to Premier Edouard Daladier and Foreign Minister Georges Bonnet. In addition, Bullitt was in frequent contact with Joseph Kennedy, the American ambassador in London, who could relay Beck's views to the British government.

Much of Biddle's long and rambling report, based on his conversations with Beck and other highly placed Polish officials, deals with Poland's attitude toward Germany, particularly its opposition to the possibility of German expansion into the Ukraine via Czechoslovakia through Subcarpathian Ruthenia. It also shows that Beck did not envisage playing into German hands; on the contrary, Biddle stresses the deep apprehension of "Polish officialdom" about the potential German threat to the Corridor, Danzig, and Polish Upper Silesia. Therefore, Biddle thought that Poland would increasingly recognize the potential for conflict with Germany. He reported a deep-seated, though undisclosed, desire among Polish officials to prevent Czechoslovakia from becoming "a German arrow pointing too far east and running along the southern border of Poland, thus allowing for a direct and dreaded contact between Germany and the Polish Ukraine minority"—meaning the Ukrainians of former East Galicia. The Germans might use this minority both to pressure Poland and to infiltrate the Soviet Ukraine. Biddle thought that these fears motivated Polish hopes to establish "a close tie-in" with the Slovak minority in Czechoslovakia, which might strengthen Hungary and, thus, block Germany's infiltration of all of Czechoslovakia. The Poles also feared German penetration of Romania.

Biddle reported that Beck told him that if Germany failed to acquire the Ukraine through "peaceful penetration," Poland might be forced to fight to prevent German troops from transiting its territory. In this case, Beck believed that Poland would be defeated. At least, however, Poland would first delay and "bleed" Germany, so that, eventually, thanks to Polish resistance combined with an Anglo–French clash with Germany in the west, Germany would fail to attain its objective.

In summarizing the views of Germany in Polish official circles, Biddle stated that: they expected Germany to direct its expansion toward the Black Sea, Istanbul, and beyond; and they saw Britain's role as "an honest broker" in trying to liquidate the Spanish and Czechoslovak problems as the first stage leading to a possible Anglo–German settlement—a part of Britain's ambitious program for European appeasement. In this connection, Polish officials noted Chamberlain's efforts to prevent an explosion on the continent (hence, the British pressure on France and Czechoslovakia) and to prevent Soviet participation in it.

Yet Polish officials also foresaw the possibility that Britain would adopt an alternative course. If the settlement at which Chamberlain aimed failed, he could then prove to world opinion and, more important, to public opinion in Britain and its dominions, that he had left no stone unturned in his efforts to improve relations with Germany. If he then developed a counterpolicy, Polish officials saw a chance for Poland to play a key role, possibly in forming a neutral Baltic–Black Sea or even a Baltic–Aegean axis (that is, the Third Europe), designed to thwart Germany's drive eastward. In such an eventuality, however, Poland would require clear assurances of ample British, French, and, possibly, Italian support, and would expect at least Britain and France to share any burden of responsibility that the states of eastern and central Europe might incur in provoking German ire.

Warsaw was not overly concerned about French anger at Polish policy, for they realized that France must follow Britain. In this regard, Biddle noted Beck's hope of eventually linking Poland's forceful action in countering German expansionist ambitions with that of France and Britain. Beck suggested that this might be the best way for Poland to avoid the grim prospect of either becoming a potential victim of German expansion or serving as a pathway for German expansion to the Ukraine. Biddle concluded: "I should look for Poland to be fighting on the side of Britain and France in the event they came to blows with Germany."

As for Polish views on Czechoslovakia, Biddle reported that a German-infiltrated Czechoslovakia would be for Poland "like one's trying to sleep peacefully with a strand of barbed-wire at the foot of one's bed." Here he wrote:

> Beck, moreover, is aware that the combined armies of Poland, her ally Romania, possibly Yugoslavia and Hungary, and even Czechoslovakia, would potentially present an effective resistance to a German eastward military action, provided the British and French forces simultaneously engaged the Germans on the German Western Front. Though Poland and Czechoslovakia, fighting side by side might form incongruous military bedmates, their geopolitical positions are at least vis-à-vis Germany similar, and an actual German aggression might conceivably throw them on the same side, particularly if Poland were assured of synchronous [sic] forceful action on the part of Britain and France in the West. Besides, in such an event, Poland would march not for Czechoslovakia, but against Germany.[27]

This passage clearly indicates that if France and Britain decided to fight for Czechoslovakia and committed themselves to military action against Germany in the West, then Poland would join them at Czechoslovakia's side, perhaps with the aid of Romania and Yugoslavia.

Because Beck rarely shared his thoughts with anyone but his most trusted colleagues, the details of his views, as reported by Noël on 26 April, might have been a conscious effort by the Polish foreign minister to sound out France, and, perhaps, Britain as well, on possible solutions to the Czechoslovak crisis. There was no French reaction to these suggestions, however, and Bonnet's belated reply to Beck's proposal of 24 May that France and Poland might discuss all "new phenomena" in central Europe (obviously, the Czechoslovak crisis) was deemed inadequate;[28] he may have hoped that Biddle's report would evoke a more positive response. Thus, the views ascribed by Biddle to Polish officials, and especially to Beck, were probably designed to reach French and British ears and to learn whether they were interested either in supporting a future east European bloc or in offering military support in 1938 to Poland, Czechoslovakia, and, possibly, Romania and Yugoslavia, against Germany. It is not known whether these ideas were relayed to the French and British governments in the summer of 1938, but, if they were, they must not have been thought worth considering. There is no documentary evidence to suggest otherwise. Nevertheless, a similar statement on Polish policy was transmitted later to London through another channel. On 31 August, Sir Robert Vansittart, then chief diplomatic adviser to the Foreign Office, noted a statement from a member of Marshal Śmigły-Rydz's entourage that Polish policy would depend on the Western Powers—if they helped Czechoslovakia, Poland would fight alongside them; if they did not, Poland would annex its share of Czechoslovakia.[29]

From June to September 1938, Poland kept its options open. Beck also tried to obtain German recognition of the Free City of Danzig and an extension of the German–Polish declaration of nonaggression in return for Polish "neutrality." He failed, however, because Hitler clearly saw no need to pay this price.[30]

And now to the last days of September 1938. Western leaders capitulated to Hitler at the Munich Conference, which ended in the early morning hours of 30 September. Beck had expected to be invited to the conference—via Mussolini—but this did not happen.[31] Furthermore, although Czechoslovakia was to relinquish the Sudetenland, Polish and Hungarian claims were postponed for future settlement, as was the finalization of the Franco–British guarantee for Czechoslovakia. Finally, we know that the Czechoslovak government was told by the French and British ministers that, if it refused to accept the Munich decisions, it would be left to its own devices. Prague gave its official assent at 12:30 P.M. on 30 September.

Eleven hours later, at 11:40 that evening, the Polish minister in Prague, Kazimierz Papée, delivered an ultimatum from his government to Czechoslovak Foreign Minister Krofta. The ultimatum rejected Prague's agreement in principle to Polish demands to hand over Zaolzie and its proposal of negotiations. Instead, Warsaw demanded immediate agreement to the cession of the preponderantly Polish areas of Zaolzie to Poland and left other areas open for negotiation.[32] In fact, the Czechoslovak government had declared in early May that it would grant the same concessions to the Polish minority as it would to any other—in this case, the Germans. An addition, during late September, both the British and French governments exerted pressure on President Beneš to agree to Polish demands in return for Polish neutrality, while after Munich they advised that the matter be settled to Poland's satisfaction, but by negotiation.[33] What is not known, however, is that before sending the ultimatum, the Polish decision makers briefly considered mobilizing in support of Czechoslovakia—if the latter decided to resist rather than accept the decisions of the Munich Conference.

This astonishing information comes from the unpublished memoirs of Michał Łubieński, Beck's "Chef de Cabinet," who was in close daily contact with the foreign minister. In these memoirs, written either during or after the war, Łubieński recalls:

> In Warsaw, the news of this agreement [Munich] caused consternation. After all, the Czechs were our Slavic neighbor, and the strengthening of the German state and its [new] location south of us could not find us indifferent. Finally, what was most painful for Beck's great power diplomacy in a matter of such vital concern to us in this central European matter, an understanding was concluded by the Four Powers at the expense of our small neighbor without consulting Poland and without securing her agreement. We were betrayed by our ally France and by friendly Germany, not to mention England and Italy. . . .
>
> Munich provoked such general indignation in Poland that we feared mob assaults on the French embassy, and particularly on the British embassy; we also feared demonstrations against the government.
>
> When the news arrived that evening [sic] Beck called me in to see him and we spent a long time discussing whether we should mobilize in defense of Czechoslovakia. Beck also discussed this matter with the chief of [the general] staff. Finally, we heard the decision: "This could have been done if there had been certainty that the Czechs wanted to fight." And yet not only was this certainty lacking, but our information led us to conclude that the Czechs would break down completely.
>
> We took the path of recovering Zaolzie. It was a scrap of booty, thrown [to us] by way of consolation.[34]

Although there is no confirmation of Łubieński's dramatic account of the deliberations of whether Poland should mobilize to help Czechoslovakia, this decision clearly depended on whether Prague would fight rather than accept the Munich decisions, and, therefore, on the corollary assumption that, if it fought, France would be forced to fulfill its obligations and Britain would support it. Poland would then align itself with Czechoslovakia and the Western Powers against Germany. We should note that this attitude was in line with Beck's statement as reported by Biddle in June, the statement made by a member of Marshal Śmigły-Rydz's entourage as noted by Vansittart, Beck's statement to

Biddle, and, finally, with the statement he claims to have made at a castle conference in 1938. This statement maintained that if his basic hypothesis were disproved by events, if France and Britain came out in support of Czechoslovakia, Poland must turn around its policy within twenty-four hours, because it could not fight on Germany's side.

Łubieński was not an unquestioning admirer of Beck's policies; indeed, he was critical of them and appeared to have no interest in defending Beck in his memoirs. As for Łubieński's remarks on Beck's Great Power policy, one must remember that the foreign minister always denied that Poland was a power on the scale of France and Britain, but said that it was a power to be reckoned with in central Europe. On a European scale, he believed that its status was based on the fact that no moves or decisions could be contemplated without its participation.[35] Hence, the agreement reached at Munich, without Poland, was truly a bitter blow.

Beck apparently first heard about the Munich decisions in the early hours of 30 September. At 8 o'clock in the morning, the Polish foreign ministry received a cipher telegram from Papée in Prague, which reported that the latter had accepted the Franco–British proposals in principle, although with numerous reservations.[36] The official Czechoslovak acceptance was announced at 12:30 P.M. that day.

A meeting of the inner cabinet took place at the Royal Castle on 30 September, probably in the early afternoon after receiving news of Prague's definitive acceptance of the Munich decisions. We read in Szembek's diary:

> *Conversation with Beck* (at 14:30 in the presence of director Łubieński). The minister informed us that in view of the Munich Conference, where an effort was made by the directory of the great powers to impose binding decisions on other states (to which Poland cannot agree, for she would then be reduced to the role of a political object directed by others according to their will), and also in view of Czechoslovakia's failure to meet our demands, a special conference took place today at the [residence] of the president of the Republic. Apart from the president and the minister [of foreign affairs], the participants were Marshal Śmigły, Premier Sławoj-Składkowski, and Minister Kwiatkowski. At this conference, it was decided that we should put our demands to Prague categorically and as an ultimatum. If this does not work, military steps will be taken. The minister then showed us a sketch of his note to the Prague government and asked that it be completed immediately. It is to be sent to Prague by plane today, so

that Minister Papée can deliver it before midnight. The deadline for their answer expires at noon tomorrow when our troops will immediately enter Teschen.[37]

So much for Szembek. It was not until many years later that an account emerged of the castle conference as related by one of its participants. It is included in a portrait of Józef Beck that was written in the 1960s by former Deputy Premier and Finance Minister Eugeniusz Kwiatkowski. It was first published in an underground Polish periodical in 1985 and reprinted in Paris in 1986. Kwiatkowski's account is important for, although written many years after the event, it enumerates Beck's arguments in favor of the ultimatum in a manner typical of his style and reasoning.[38]

Beck prefaced his statement by listing Polish grievances against Czechoslovakia. After enumerating them, Kwiatkowski writes that Beck also put forward arguments of a political-tactical nature for sending an ultimatum to Prague. Kwiatkowski writes that Beck

claimed—not without justice—that what had happened at Munich, and was reminiscent of the plan for a "Four Power Pact" of a few years ago, could become a very dangerous precedent also in regard to Poland's vital interests. We should—in his view—quickly and quite drastically take a stand against such methods of resolving territorial conflicts [by] evoking the phantom of a war which is not very likely [to occur] in this case. Only such a determined and courageous step by Poland can save it from a new Munich. Furthermore, the close geographic proximity of Germany forces Poland to take immediate action. If we hesitate and delay, Germany may seize this valuable and highly industrialized patch of land, eliminating Polish claims to Zaolzie for a long time to come. Finally, said Beck, we have long been demanding, and have received, the Czechoslovak government's agreement in principle to the equal treatment of the Polish claims and the rights granted by Czechoslovakia to its German minority. Today, when the Prague government is ceding to the Reich territories inhabited by Germans, and this with the approval of the Western Powers, we must resolutely demand an analogous solution to Poland's small but justified claim.

Kwiatkowski goes on to say that all of the participants in the castle conference agreed in principle with Beck's arguments. There was a sharp clash, however, when Kwiatkowski opposed presenting the Polish demand as an ultimatum. He believed that the timing was singularly inopportune because it would appear as though Poland were cooperating with the Nazi aggressor against Czechoslovakia. He appealed for the use of normal diplomatic procedures in a calm and businesslike atmosphere, because Poland's goals should be to prevent the public's identification of Polish actions with German behavior, and not to appear to be acting either too precipitously or disharmoniously with Poland's western friends. Finally, Kwiatkowski warned against creating a dangerous pretext for intervention by the Soviet Union, which was linked by a conditional treaty of mutual assistance with Czechoslovakia (conditional upon France's first coming to the aid of Czechoslovakia).

According to Kwiatkowski, Marshal Śmigły-Rydz violently opposed these arguments. Beck ignored the first two and did not answer the third, although he was in possession of a sharp and somewhat ambivalent Soviet note of 22 September, which he did not disclose to the others.[39] That same day, the Polish ultimatum was sent to Prague.[40]

It is true, of course, that a small Polish army corps had been hastily assembled on the Polish–Czechoslovak border on 23 September.[41] This date coincided with the results of the Hitler–Chamberlain conversations at Godesberg on 22–23 September, in which Britain rejected Hitler's expanded demands (which now included Polish and Hungarian claims), and the Franco–British message to Prague that the two powers had no objection to Czechoslovak mobilization, which then took place. The crisis passed with Hitler's acceptance of Chamberlain's proposal for a conference, which Mussolini had transmitted as his own.

Finally, it should be noted that on 28 September, when it was already known that the Western Powers would meet with Hitler and Mussolini, the Polish government learned that on the map presented by Hitler to Chamberlain at Godesberg, the northwestern part of Zaolzie (which included significant coal mines and steel industry as well as the important railway junction of Bohumin) was destined to go to Germany. This is probably what Beck had in mind when he said at the Warsaw castle conference of 30 September that Germany might seize the area. The Polish government then demanded the whole region through its ambassador in Berlin, Józef Lipski. Hitler agreed to this, against the wishes of Göring and German military leaders. Indeed, on 1 October, Lipski reported Göring's suggestion that plebiscites be held in the Polish-speaking part of the Frydek region (for or against Poland) and in Moravska–Ostrava (for or against Germany). This suggestion was rejected by Warsaw. Five days later, Beck informed Lipski that preliminary preparations were being made by Poland for Polish railway workers to occupy the Bohumin railway station in preparation for the entry of Polish troops. The Polish–German dispute over Bohumin was finally settled on 8 October, and, two days later, it was occupied by Polish troops.[42] Thus, at the same time that he was negotiating with Berlin, Beck was prepared to risk a clash with it over Bohumin.

What might have happened had Czechoslovakia decided to fight rather than accept the decisions made at Munich? What if France had then declared war on Germany (presumably with British support)? What if Poland had fought on the side of Czechoslovakia, as Beck had envisaged in his talks with Bullitt in June 1938, and considered again, briefly, on 30 September?[43] Of course, these are purely hypothetical questions, because it is most unlikely that President Beneš, realizing that the French would only man the Maginot Line, while the Soviets would not make a move, would have rejected the Munich agreement and, thereby, exposed his country and his people to what he believed was inevitable destruction.

As we know today, the French general staff believed that France could do nothing more than mobilize its army (which would take fifteen days), man the Maginot Line, and seize a few strips of German territory as a *prise des gages* (forfeit). Thus, the only thing they thought they could do to help Czechoslovakia, whether or not Poland, Romania, and Yugoslavia helped, was to tie down a part of the German army on the Franco–German frontier.[44] This, of course, was exactly what France did in September 1939 after the German attack on Poland—a strategy resulting in the *Drôle de Guerre*, the phony war. It can, therefore, be assumed that, even in the unlikely event that Czechoslovakia had fought and Poland had come into the war on Prague's side, the two would have fought alone. They undoubtedly would have fought valiantly, but they could not have prevailed against Germany.

Finally, Soviet aid for Czechoslovakia appeared dubious at best. We know that Beneš considered Soviet assurances of aid. Years later, he claimed privately that Moscow was just as guilty of abandoning Czechoslovakia as were France and Britain.[45] It is true that on 22 September, with Beneš's prodding, the Soviet Union threatened to abrogate the Polish–Soviet nonaggression pact if Polish troops marched into Czechoslovakia, but it did not do so. Would Moscow have marched to the aid of Prague had the latter fought rather than accepted the Munich decisions, and had Poland then lined up with Czechoslovakia?

There can be no complete answer to this question until Soviet archives covering this period are opened. There are indications, however, that it was equally unlikely for Stalin to have risked a war with Germany in 1938 as in 1939. Hence, one can assume that if Czechoslovakia had fought and France had been at war with Germany (in the same way that it would be in 1939), Stalin would most likely have bargained with

Hitler over Poland, and possibly other countries, as he actually would do a year later. This type of policy is indicated by Moscow's advice of caution when Beneš asked for Soviet support for his letter of 22 September to President Mościcki offering negotiations. In reporting this advice, the Czechoslovak minister in Moscow, Zdenek Fierlinger, added his expectation that, in the event of a "favorable development," the Soviet Union would attempt to establish a common border with Czechoslovakia. He wrote that the Soviets "are resolved not to leave Warsaw's behavior toward us without punishment. They do not doubt that the hour of reckoning will arrive."[46] Of course, a common Soviet–Czechoslovak border could be established only through a Soviet annexation of southeastern Poland (former East Galicia), which Stalin did—along with the rest of eastern Poland—in September 1939.

Thus, this annexation could have formed part of a Soviet–German deal in September 1938, which most probably would have included Soviet assent to the German annexation of the Sudetenland. This possibility is indicated, not only by Fierlinger's assessment, but also by the Soviets' official declarations of noninvolvement in the peace settlements of 1919 and their support for self-determination during the crisis, which facilitated the German annexation of the Sudetenland and a German–Soviet agreement partitioning Poland. This possibility is further indicated by the fact that Moscow completely ignored the personal letter of 24 September from Romanian Foreign Minister Nicolae Petrescu-Comnen to Soviet Foreign Minister Maxim Litvinov, although the two ministers had been conducting talks in Geneva. In the name of his government, Comnen offered Soviet troops passage to Czechoslovakia through a piece of strictly defined Romanian territory should war break out. Furthermore, Romania agreed to allow Soviet planes to fly over its territory. Finally, Comnen specifically stated that Romania required no Soviet guarantees regarding Bessarabia—territory to which the Soviet Union had not relinquished its claim—or the Romanian–Hungarian frontier in Transylvania (where, as elsewhere, the Comintern had proclaimed its adherence to the principle of self-determination, which meant the division of Transylvania). Thus, Romania was willing to permit the transit of Soviet troops and planes in the event that the Soviet Union decided to assist Czechoslovakia in a war.[47]

If Soviet historians should some day acknowledge the Romanian offer, they could argue that it was valid only in the event of war, which the Munich Conference prevented. But, in that case, they will also have to admit the falsity of their earlier claims that the Soviet Union had been unable to help Czechoslovakia because Poland and Romania had refused to agree to the passage of Soviet troops. We know that Bucharest had responded positively to Moscow's proposal, although in September 1938 no similar request was made of Warsaw. Finally, there were no signs of Soviet readiness for war in September 1938.

Thus, had Czechoslovakia fought, had France entered the war with Germany (presumably with British support), and had Poland then lined up with Czechoslovakia, the two states would have received no effective military help from the Western Powers, just as Poland was given none in September 1939. We can only guess what Stalin's policy would have been if the war had begun in September 1938. But, considering that Stalin did not want to risk war with Germany and that he had made overtures to Hitler in 1935 as well as 1936–37, it is quite possible that he would have tried to reach an agreement with Hitler in 1938.[48] We can only hope that glasnost will fully open the Soviet diplomatic archives. For the time being, however, Stalin cannot be viewed as having been any more heroic in 1938 than either Daladier or Chamberlain.

Finally, Poland played only a secondary role in the Munich crisis and, whatever moral judgment one makes, its government at least followed a policy that was both flexible and consistent. This policy was in accordance not only with the principles of its policy-making elite, but also with the views of most of the political parties and public opinion on the subject of Zaolzie. Undoubtedly, it would have been far better for Polish–Czechoslovak relations had Poland tried to secure its aims through negotiations rather than with an ultimatum. Considering Hitler's policy, however, it is unlikely that such negotiations would have succeeded. Therefore, if Poland had not secured its demands through the ultimatum, it would most probably have had to accept Zaolzie as a gift from Hitler, and Henri Rollet may well be correct in suggesting that the führer would have used this gift to gain territorial concessions from Poland.[49] Either way, the developments of 1939 clearly demonstrate that neither the ultimatum nor negotiations over Zaolzie would have saved Czechoslovakia in 1938. Nor, indeed, could Poland have been preserved from the avalanche that would begin, ostensibly over Danzig, one year later.

NOTES

1. See Anna M. Cienciala, *Poland and the Western Powers 1938–1939. A Study in the Interdependence of Eastern and Western Europe* (London, 1968), chaps. 1–4; and Cienciala, "Poland and the Munich Crisis, 1938, a Reappraisal," *East European Quarterly* 3, no. 12 (1969): 201–19.
2. See map "Cieszyn Silesia. Language Boundary" in Bogusław Kożusznik, *The Problem of Cieszyn Silesia: Facts and Documents* (London, 1943), map follows p. 58; see also map in Cienciala, *Poland*, following p. 292.
3. On the local Polish–Czech agreement of 5 November 1918, Piłsudski's proposal, and the events of 1919–20, see Piotr S. Wandycz, *France and Her Eastern Allies 1919–1925.*

French–Czechoslovak–Polish Relations from the Paris Peace Conference to Locarno (Minneapolis, 1962), chap. 3 and map facing p. 76.

4. On the Polish government's belief that Prague was the center of Comintern activity in central Europe, Warsaw's "Comintern note" to Prague of 2 March and Prague's answer, as well as information about Polish communists in Zaolzie, see Józef Kowalczyk, *Za kulisami wydarzeń politycznych z lat 1936–1938* (Behind the scenes of the political events of 1936–38) (Warsaw, 1976). See also Stefania Stanisławska, *Wielka i mała polityka Józefa Becka* (Józef Beck's great and little policy) (Warsaw, 1962), 85ff, in Cienciala, *Poland*, 61. The PCP was dissolved by Stalin sometime in 1938.

5. For the Fiala report of 28 April 1938, see Stanisławska, *Wielka i mała polityka*, 110ff, in Cienciala, *Poland*, 66–69.

6. On Beneš's support for German revisionist claims against Poland in the Weimar period, see Wandycz, *France 1919–1925*, 336–37; on Masaryk to G. Stresemann for the same subject, see F. Gregory Campbell, *Confrontations in Central Europe. Weimar Germany and Czechoslovakia* (Chicago, 1975), 182–83.

7. On Polish attempts at closer relations with Czechoslovakia in the period 1925–33, see Wandycz, *France 1919–1925*, chaps. 9–10, and Wandycz, *The Twilight of French Eastern Alliances, 1926–1936. French–Czechoslovak–Polish Relations from Locarno to the Remilitarization of the Rhineland* (Princeton, N.J., 1988), chaps. 3, 9, 10; see also J. Kozeński, *Czechosłowacja w polskiej polityce zagranicznej w latach 1932–1938* (Czechoslovakia in Poland's foreign policy, 1932–38) (Poznań, 1964).

8. As Arnost Heidrich, secretary of the Czechoslovak foreign ministry, stated in a note dated 15 June 1938, when Beck tried in 1933 to explore the possibility of a Polish–Czechoslovak alliance, Prague rejected this concept, viewing Poland as more threatened by German aggression than Czechoslovakia. See Stanisławska, *Wielka i mała polityka*, 12–14, in Wandycz, *Twilight*, 282.

9. See Jules Laroche's report of 19 December 1933, *Documents Diplomatiques Français* (henceforth: *DDF*), 1st ser., 5, no. 156.

10. For Polish views of the Locarno Treaties, especially of the Franco–Polish Mutual Assistance Treaty, see Wandycz, *France 1919–1925*, chap. 13; and Anna M. Cienciala and Titus Komarnicki, *From Versailles to Locarno. Keys to Polish Foreign Policy 1919–1925* (Lawrence, Kan., 1984), chap. 10.

11. See Anna M. Cienciala, "Polish Foreign Policy, 1926–1939: 'Equilibrium,' Stereotype and Reality," *Polish Review* 22, no. 1 (1975): 42–58. For a major study on this subject, see Michal J. Zacharias, *Polska wobec zmian w układzie sił politycznych w Europie w latach 1932–1936* (Poland and the changes in the European balance of power, 1932–36) (Wrocław, 1981).

12. On Piłsudski's questions and opinions in the spring of 1934, see Cienciala, *Poland*, 34 and 57; see more extensive treatment in Wandycz, *Twilight*, 325–26.

13. On British views, see Anna M. Cienciala, "German Propaganda for the Revision of the Polish–German Frontier in Danzig and the Corridor: Its Effects on British Opinion and the British Foreign Policy-making Elite in the Years 1919–1933," *Antemurale* XX (Rome, 1976): 77–129.

14. On French attempts to water down the Franco–Polish military convention of 1921, especially the 1927 mission to Warsaw of Marshal Louis Franchet d'Espérey, see Wandycz, *Twilight*, 98ff.

15. See Anna M. Cienciala, "Poland in British and French Policy in 1939: Determination to Fight or Avoid War," *Polish Review* XXIV, no. 3 (1989): 199–226.

16. For Bonnet's statement to Osuský of 20 July 1938, see *DDF*, 2d. ser., 10, no. 238: 437–38.

17. Beck did not trust Kwiatkowski, so the latter may not have attended all the meetings. In any case, how many of these meetings actually took place is unknown.

18. On Beck's ideas for a Third Europe, see Cienciala, *Poland*, 55–176. We should note that on 20 September, Ciano, on Mussolini's instructions, had advised the Polish ambassador in Rome that Poland should make the loudest demands possible. He had, he said, advised the Hungarian minister to do the same, for Italy absolutely wanted

to see common frontiers established among Poland, Hungary, Yugoslavia, and Italy. For this perspective, see Stanislaw Sierpowski, *Stosunki polsko-włoskie w latach 1918–1940* (Polish–Italian relations in 1918–40), 5 (Warsaw, 1975), 550–52.

19. For Beck's account of his statement at the two castle conferences, see Colonel Józef Beck, *Dernier Rapport. Politique polonaise 1926–1939* (Paris and Neuchâtel, 1951), 162–63; for the Polish original, see Józef Beck, *Ostatni raport* (The last memorandum) (Warsaw, 1987), 147–48, and *Polska polityka zagraniczna w latach 1926–1939. Na podstawie tekstów min. Józefa Becka opracowała Anna M. Cienciala* (Polish foreign policy, 1926–39. The writings of Minister Józef Beck, edited and annotated by Anna M. Cienciala) (Paris, 1990), 214–15.

20. See Kazimierz Papée to Krofta, 23 March 1938, in Papée's report of 1 April 1938 in Z. Landau and J. Tomaszewski, eds., *Monachium 1938. Polskie dokumenty dyplomatyczne* (Munich 1938. Polish diplomatic documents), 27 (Warsaw, 1985). Papée probably referred to his report of 16 February 1937; see Kozeński, *Czechosłowacja*, 237.

21. For Lord Halifax's report on his visit to Germany, 17–21 November, see *Documents on British Foreign Policy, 1919–1939*, 2d ser., 19, no. 336, pp. 540–55; on Danzig, Austria, Czechoslovakia to Hitler, p. 545; for Szembek's note on information from Berlin, see Tytus Komarnicki, ed., *Diariusz i teki Jana Szembeka (1935–1945)* (Jan Szembek's diary and papers), 3 (London, 1969), 3 December 1937, p. 200; on Beck's conversations in Berlin, 13–14 January 1938, see Waclaw Jedrzejewicz, ed., *Diplomat in Berlin 1933–1939. Papers and Memoirs of Józef Lipski, Ambassador of Poland* (New York, 1968), 321–38; for the original Polish documents, see *Monachium 1938*, no. 1.

22. Cited in Kazimierz Wierzbiański, "Czechy a Polska" (Czechoslovakia and Poland), *Niepodległość* (London and New York, 1952), 4, 99.

23. For Neville Chamberlain's statements on Czechoslovakia in the House of Commons on 24 March 1938, see *Parliamentary Debates. House of Commons*, 5th ser., col. 1405.

24. See *Monachium*, no. 27.

25. For Noël's report of 26 April 1938, see *DDF*, 2d ser., 9, no. 248, pp. 533–34.

26. For the Szembek–R. Raczyński conversation of 18 April 1938 and Szembek's instructions, see Józef Zarański, ed., *DiT,* 4 (London, 1972): 133.

27. For Drexel Biddle's report of 19 June 1938, see Philip V. Cannistraro, Edward D. Wynot, Jr., and Theodore P. Kovaleff, eds., *Poland and the Coming of the Second World War. The Diplomatic Papers of A. J. Drexel Biddle, Jr., United States Ambassador to Poland 1937–1939* (Columbus, Ohio, 1976), doc. 4, pp. 208ff. This document was not published in the *Foreign Relations of the United States, 1938.*

We know that both Piłsudski and Beck refused earlier to respond to German hints about a joint Polish–German crusade against the USSR, following which Poland would be compensated for making concessions to Germany with land in the Ukraine. For Piłsudski's refusal to discuss a common Polish–German attack on the USSR and partition of the Ukraine, see Jules Laroche, *La Pologne de Piłsudski. Souvenirs d'une ambassade, 1926–1933* (Piłsudski's Poland. Memoirs from an embassy, 1926–1933) (Paris, 1953), 194; see also the December 1933 German document cited in Gerhard L. Weinberg, *The Foreign Policy of Hitler's Germany. Diplomatic Revolution in Europe, 1933–1936* (Chicago, 1970), 71; also Anna M. Cienciala, "Marxism and History," *East European Quarterly* 6, no. 1 (1972): 104. There is no evidence in either German or Polish documents that Beck ever agreed to discuss a common Polish–German march on the USSR and a partition of the Ukraine.

28. For Beck's proposal to discuss "new phenomena" and Bonnet's delayed reply, see Cienciala, *Poland*, 76–77, 83. For the reports of the Polish ambassador in Paris on the same subjects, see Wacław Jędrzejewicz, ed., *Diplomat in Paris 1936–1939. Papers and Memoirs of Juliusz Łukasiewicz Ambassador of Poland* (New York, 1970), pp. 53ff; original Polish documents in *Monachium 1938.*

29. For Vansittart's note of 31 August 1938, see Gerhard L. Weinberg, *The Foreign Policy of Hitler's Germany. Starting World War II, 1937–1939* (Chicago, 1980), 402, note 102. The same information is given retrospectively by Wierzbiański, who also adds that if the Czechoslovak government fought and left Prague, the Polish minister would

accompany it. See Kazimierz Wierzbiański, "Benesz a Polska," *Zeszyty Historyczne*, no. 76 (Paris, 1986): 82.

30. For Polish efforts to secure German recognition of the Free City of Danzig and an extension of the declaration of nonaggression in the first part of September 1938, and their failure, see Cienciala, *Poland*, 105–106, and Jędrzejewicz, *Diplomat in Berlin*, 393–400; original Polish documents in *Monachium 1938*.

31. Poland's ambassador to Italy, Bolesław Wieniawa-Długoszowski, expected Mussolini to support Poland's participation in the conference, and said that he approved Polish demands on Czechoslovakia. For Ciano's promise of Italian help, see Sierpowski, *Stosunki polsko-włoskie*, 550–51. Because both Chamberlain and Daladier were opposed, however, Hitler did not insist.

32. For the Polish ultimatum of 30 September 1938, see Szembek, *DiT*, 4: 444–46 (French text); and *Monachium 1938*, 449.

33. For Prague's declaration of 4 May 1938 made by Minister Juraj Slavik to Beck, that the same concessions would be made to the Polish minority as to the German one, see *Poland*, 72, and *Monachium*, no. 55, 103. On British and French support for Polish demands and pressure on Prague to grant them, as well as their subsequent advice to resolve the issue by negotiation, see ibid., p. 131ff, and Anna M. Cienciala, "Poland and the Munich Crisis, 1938," *East European Quarterly* 3, no. 2 (1969): 207, note 24. See also *DDF*, 2d ser, 11, nos. 432, 440, 491, 498, 500, 502–507, 512.

34. See Michał Łubieński, *Refleksje i reminiscensje* (Reflections and reminiscences), typescript, archives of the Józef Piłsudski Institute of America, New York, trans. A.M. Cienciala, p. 67.

35. See, for example, Szembek's note of 10 January 1938, Szembek, *DiT,* 4: 11.

36. See *Monachium 1938*, no. 435.

37. On Beck's statement and instruction to Szembek of 30 September 1938, 2:30 P.M., see Szembek, *DiT,* 4: 283–84.

38. Examples of Beck's style can be found both in his memoirs and in Szembek's diary.

39. See Eugeniusz Kwiatkowski, "Józef Beck," *Arka* (Cracow) no. 12, 1985; reprinted in *Zeszyty Historyczne* 76 (Paris, 1986): 14–32; on the castle conference of 30 September 1938, see ibid., 27–28 (on 27, the date is misprinted as 13 Sept). For the Soviet note to Poland of 23 September and Beck's reply on the same day, see Szembek, *DiT,* 4: 436–37; reprinted in *Monachium 1938*, nos. 282 and 289. It is likely that only Kwiatkowski had not been informed of the Polish–Soviet exchange.

40. See Szembek, *DiT,* 4, 444–46; *Monachium*, no. 449.

41. This was the *Samodzielna grupa operacyjna Śląsk* (Autonomous operations group Silesia), on whose activities a typed report is preserved in the archives of the Józef Piłsudski Institute of America, New York; also cited in Cienciala, *Poland*, 135, note 94.

42. On the Godesberg map, German claims, Polish reaction and negotiations, see Cienciala, *Poland*, 136–38, 149–52.

43. See Michał Łubieński's memoirs, note 34.

44. For French military plans in 1938, see *DDF*, 2d ser., 8, nos. 442, 446, 462, and 9, no. 73; see also Colonel Pierre le Goyet, *Munich. "Un traquenard?"* (Paris, 1988), 118ff. Le Goyet's book was ready many years earlier, but French military authorities had prohibited its publication; unfortunately, the author and his editors did not update the footnotes to include documents for 1938 published in the volumes cited above.

45. For Soviet policy toward Czechoslovakia in 1938, see Jiří Hochman, *The Soviet Union and the Failure of Collective Security, 1934–1938* (Ithaca, 1984), chap. 7, as well as the chapter on the role of President Edvard Beneš in the Munich Crisis, printed in this volume; for Beneš's 1945 statement on Soviet policy in 1938, see Edward Táborský, *President Edvard Beneš between East and West, 1938–1948* (Stanford, 1981), 62.

46. For Fierlinger's report of 23 September 1938, see Hochman, *The Soviet Union*, 165.

47. See Note of the Romanian Government to the Government of the Soviet Union, Geneva, Bucharest, 24 September 1938 (French text), in Hochman, *The Soviet Union*, app. C, 194–201. The letter is addressed by Nicolae Petrescu-Comnen to Maxim

Litvinov at Geneva. Comnen stated that in view of the Czechoslovak mobilization of 23 September, undertaken with the knowledge of the French and British governments, the Czechoslovak crisis had entered its final stage. It is noteworthy that the Romanian government specifically renounced any claim to Soviet guarantees for the territorial inviolability of Romania. Soviet land transit was limited to a small strip of territory, which contained the only railway line between Cernauti and Negresti; the Romanian government also set a time limit for Soviet land and air traffic through its territory to Czechoslovakia (12 days beginning on 25 September). Litvinov left Geneva for Moscow on 24 September.

48. For Soviet proposals of a Nazi German nonaggression pact, see Schulenburg, Report of 8 May 1935, *Documents on German Foreign Policy*, ser. C, 4, no. 78; also Hjalmar Schacht to von Neurath, 6 February 1937, and von Neurath to Schacht, 11 February 1937, ibid., 6, nos. 183, 195.

49. See Henri Rollet, *La Pologne au XX siècle* (Paris, 1984), 304.

ABOUT THE AUTHORS

Anna M. Cienciala received a Ph.D. with specialization in Modern East Central Europe from Indiana University, and is currently Professor of East European History and Soviet and East European Studies at the University of Kansas in Lawrence, Kansas. She is the author of *Poland and the Western Powers, 1938–39: A Study in the Interdependence of Eastern and Western Europe,* and, with Titus Komarnicki, *From Versailles to Locarno: Keys to Polish Foreign Policy, 1919–25.* Her most recent work is an annotated Polish edition of the diplomatic notes of Józef Beck, Polish Foreign Minister 1932–39, published by the Institut Littéraire, Paris, 1980.

John E. Dreifort is Chair of the Department of History at Wichita State University. Professor Dreifort was educated at Bowling Green State University (B.A. and M.A.) and received his Ph.D. in Modern European History from Kent State University. His publications include *Yvon Delbas at the Quai D'Orsay, French Foreign Policy During the Popular Front, 1936–38,* and contributions to several books, including "France, Britain, and the Munich Pact: An Interim Assessment," in *Proceedings of the Western Society for the Study of French History* (1974).

Michael Kraus is Associate Professor of Political Science at Middlebury College. Professor Kraus received a B.A. from the University of Colorado, and an M.A. and Ph.D. from Princeton University. His publications include *Perestroika and East-West Economic Relations: Prospects for the 1990s* (edited with Ronald Liebowitz), *The Soviet Union and Czechoslovakia, 1938–48: The Foundations of Communist Rule, The Soviet Union Under Gorbachev: Change and Resistance, Essays in Honor of Robert C. Tucker* (with Stephen F. Cohen), and numerous articles and papers on East European and Soviet affairs.

John R. Lampe is Director of East European Studies at the Woodrow Wilson Center in Washington, D.C., since 1987, and Professor of History at the University of Maryland, College Park. He received his B.A. from Harvard University, his M.A. from the University of Minnesota, and Ph.D. in 1971 from the University of Wisconsin. He was a Foreign Service Officer in Yugoslavia and Bulgaria from 1964 to 1967. He is the author of *The Bulgarian Economy in the 20th Century* (1986), and co-author of *Balkan Economic History, 1550–1950: From Imperial Borderlands to Developing Nations* (1982), which won the Vucinich Prize of the American Association for the Advancement of Slavic Studies, and *Yugoslav–American Economic Relations since World War II* (1990).

Maya Latynski is Program Associate for East European Studies at the Woodrow Wilson International Center for Scholars. She is the translator of Adam Michnik's *Letters from Prison and Other Essays* and has written on East European and Polish affairs. She is a Ph.D. candidate in European politics at Georgetown University's Department of Government.

Gerhard L. Weinberg is William Rand Kenan, Jr., Professor of History at the University of North Carolina at Chapel Hill. Professor Weinberg has held teaching posts at the University of Michigan, the University of Kentucky, and the University of Chicago. He is the author of *The Foreign Policy of Hitler's Germany: Diplomatic Revolution in Europe, 1933–36*, for which he received the George Lewis Beer Prize of the American Historical Association in 1971, *The Foreign Policy of Hitler's Germany: Starting World War II, 1937–39*, for which he received the Halverson Prize of the Western Association of German Studies in 1981, *World in the Balance: Behind the Scenes of World War II*, and numerous journal articles. Professor Weinberg received a B.A. degree from State University of New York at Albany, and his M.A. and Ph.D. degrees from the University of Chicago.

Joseph Frederick Zacek is Professor of History at the State University of New York at Albany. He did his doctoral studies in history at the University of Illinois and Columbia (Certificate of the Institute on East Central Europe). He has taught at Occidental College and the University of California, Los Angeles, and was a visiting scholar at Columbia and the University of Illinois. He has published *Palacký: The Historian as Scholar and Nationalist*, and has authored and collaborated on other books, chapters, and articles. Currently, he is a Fellow of the Russian Research Center at Harvard, where he is working on *A Modern History of the Czechs and Slovaks*, a study commissioned by the Joint Committee on Eastern Europe of the ACLS/SSRC.

INDEX